SPEECH AND THOUGHT
IN SEVERE SUBNORMALITY

Speech and Thought

in Severe Subnormality

AN EXPERIMENTAL STUDY

N. O'CONNOR

AND

BEATE HERMELIN

Medical Research Council, Social Psychiatry Research Unit
Institute of Psychiatry
The Maudsley Hospital, London

A Pergamon Press Book

THE MACMILLAN COMPANY
NEW YORK
1963

THE MACMILLAN COMPANY
60 Fifth Avenue
New York 11, N.Y.

This book is distributed by
THE MACMILLAN COMPANY · NEW YORK
pursuant to a special arrangement with
PERGAMON PRESS LIMITED
Oxford, England

Library of Congress Card No. 62-21782

Set in 11 on 12 pt. Imprint.
Printed in Great Britain by Billing & Sons Ltd.
Guildford and London

To Professor Aubrey Lewis

CONTENTS

FOREWORD

Speech and Thought in Severe Subnormality

IT is a pleasant task for me to be able to write a few words as a foreword to this excellent book.

In pedagogics as in medicine there is an especially urgent need for a sound scientific approach. This is necessary as a basis for the education of children and also for the treatment of patients. Without objective classification of the characteristics of the perception and action, speech and thought of the child, the scientific basis of education is just as impossible as the rational treatment of disease would be without a knowledge of the nature of the illness and of the clinical state of the patient.

The teaching and education of the mentally backward child, a borderland between pedagogics and medicine, has long been delayed by an absence of careful psychophysiological investigation of the special features which distinguish these children from their normal peers. The introduction of psychometrics made it possible to orient oneself quickly to the child population and distinguish from among them any group of children who were backward in their psychological development. This was a significant step; but it could not provide an analysis of the peculiarities of perception, speech and thought which distinguish these children, and without which any constructive and scientific basis for their education is impossible. Only in the last few years has serious work devoted to this qualitative analysis of the special features of mentally handicapped children been commenced in several countries. This work proceeds along several different paths; some investigators prefer to concentrate mainly on the clinical description of the mentally backward, others on the characteristics of higher nervous activity in these children and yet others again on the peculiarities of their perceptual behaviour. It is natural that each of these lines of work makes its own contribution to the study of the mentally

handicapped child and suggests a new approach to the teaching
and education of such children.

This book by Dr. O'Connor and Dr. Hermelin is distinguished
from that of many other investigations in the field of mental
deficiency by the breadth of its scope and by the careful and
systematic nature of the experiments reported.

Including studies of perception and learning, the characteristics
of speech and thought, the formation of concepts and rote learning
in the mentally retarded child, the book covers facts relevant to
many of the essential problems of the psychology of backward
children. The approach to these problems takes into account contemporary psychophysiology on the one hand and psychological
theory on the other. The book enables the reader to recognize
how productive the investigation of old problems can be, providing
an approach is made to them with new ideas and a precise metho-
dology. Using the data obtained by investigators in other countries
and verifying these data in their own experiments as well as
putting forward their own ideas, the authors have made a contribution the significance of which will extend beyond the borders
of any one country.

If one further takes into account the humane and optimistic
approach with which these authors tackle the problem of the
education of the mentally backward, which is a very difficult
aspect of pedagogics, the importance of this book becomes clear.

No one can doubt that a reader who acquaints himself with it
will value its clarity of thought and approve of the motives which
inspired the authors in this important work.

PROFESSOR A. R. LURIA.

Moscow,
    1962

ACKNOWLEDGEMENTS

WE WOULD like to acknowledge the comments and criticisms which many colleagues have offered us concerning the form of presentation of this book. We are particularly indebted to Professor Magdalen Vernon, Professor Carolus Oldfield, Professor Oliver Zangwill, Drs. Ann and Alan Clarke and Dr. Jack Tizard.

Dr. A. E. Maxwell and Dr. P. H. Venables helped us on many occasions with the design of experiments and statistical techniques.

Our thanks are also due to the Medical Research Council, the Institute of Psychiatry and the mental deficiency hospitals in the London area which provided the facilities making these studies possible.

CHAPTER I

INTELLIGENCE AND THINKING

THIS book is about imbeciles, defined as persons who obtain intelligence test scores of between 25 and 50 I.Q. points. In our case we are concerned with imbeciles confined to mental deficiency institutions. The patients who acted as subjects in our investigations were mostly children aged from about 10 to about 16 years, though some experiments included older subjects up to the age of 30.

Having thus stated the communalities in our group, its wide diversity in other respects should not be overlooked. We are concerned with a clinically, aetiologically and behaviourally heterogeneous group of people, who all share the fate of severe impairment of their learning and thinking capacity. The reasons and mechanisms responsible for such impairment may be as diverse as the extent and location of the pathology underlying it. Our aim is the more precise analysis of the diverse processes contributing to cognitive deficits.

We recognize the value of psychometric techniques for purposes of general classification and prediction. However, as one aim of our research is to utilize existing assets to compensate for obvious deficits, this must be based on a detailed investigation of the nature of the thought processes involved. In this first chapter we are concerned with those trends and developments in the field of general psychology which are relevant to this purpose.

The concept of thought is not identical with that of intelligence. Thinking is a process conceived of as a directed skill. It is an activity and not an ability. It expresses action and not quality. There is one sense in which thinking can be considered as dependent on intelligence. There is another sense in which intelligence is defined in terms of the capacity to think, infer or for example categorize.

However, the difference between intelligence and thinking in some respects marks the difference in two psychological methods. One is concerned with the technique of measuring what any person or group can do. The other is an attempt to find out how they do it. Characteristic of the first group are the factor-analytic schools from Spearman (1927) to Thurstone (1943) and P. E. Vernon (1950) who measured and correlated abilities. Characteristic of the second are Humphrey (1948), Piaget (1955), Bartlett (1958), Bruner (1957) and Luria (1961), who have attempted to define methods of thinking used in problem solving situations. They are the successors to the line of study bugan by Binet, Simon and Vaney (1907) and by Külpe Ach, Bühler and others of the Wurzburg school. Generally speaking the lesson of the first group was that ability, once defined, determined a level of performance which could within specified limits be predicted from one test situation to another, providing the same ability was involved. Equally generally the lesson of the second group is that problem solving strategies differ, and that achievement in any one task may depend on different processes and different combinations of processes.

Woodrow (1946) who used factor analytic techniques, none the less showed that the same task was accomplished in different ways at successive stages of learning. The examination of abilities at one point in time presents a picture of their inter-relation at that moment. The examination of processes presents a more kaleido-scopic picture with the role of each ability changing in its scope and importance as skills develop. Such developmental processes present us with new entities which are not so much abilities but varying combinations of abilities. These combinations are depen-dent not only on their components as in a chemical solution but on the inter-relation of their components as in a chemical compound.

The use of a measuring and correlation technique associated with the concept of intelligence appears to have given rise to a rigid schema. The approach to problem solving and thinking appears to suggest individual differences in cognitive strategies. Bartlett (1958), discussing the possibilities of thinking of an inter-polative or extrapolative kind found that when rules of operation in a problem solving situation were not too precisely specified, several types of thinking might result, each one reaching an acceptable solution. This, of course, is in a situation when alternative choices are permissible.

The possibility of different types of thinking has long been known to child psychologists. Piaget in his many studies of children's thinking has drawn attention to the existence of different methods of thinking at different stages of mental growth.

Inhelder and Piaget (1958) distinguish different stages in the development of children's thinking. It is suggested that there is a progression with age from the first two pre-operational stages to the third, at which thinking takes place on a concrete operational level. During the pre-operational stages the child's thinking is dominated by what he directly perceives and he can be easily misled by perceptual appearances. At the concrete operational stage the child is able to make inferences about concrete material which he handles, but he is not yet able to make inferences from verbal or non-representational premises. At later ages from 7 to 14 years the transition from concrete to formal operations is made.

Piaget and Inhelder in a long series of studies have investigated the thinking and problem solving of children, examining it empirically at many different stages of growth. Their aim is to trace the development of adult thought patterns in children, basing their ideas on the assumption that formal logic provides the underlying structure for the fully developed thinking of adolescents and adults. For example, an early stage in thinking would appear to be the notion involved in the reversibility of a process. Such inversion of a process involves the associated requirement of the recognition of conservation of mass. But other changes are involved in this development toward full use of formal logic and in each it is probably Piaget's intention to show a development from concrete to formal operations or from things to propositions. Piaget suggests that the fully formal use of thinking involves the recognition of logical necessity as distinct from the "if-then" type of thinking which is common at more concrete levels.

Piaget and Inhelder, in short, show directed thinking at many different developmental levels and they show its weaknesses. Their experiments demonstrate how thought progresses from associative categories based on immediate experience to the notion of classes and class inclusion. In most instances in this work we have ingenious experiments recording the pre-suppositions apparently basic to thinking at the level involved. Either unseen objects are thought to exist no longer, or at a later stage long objects are supposed to have a greater mass than short ones or, still later, a practical solution to a reflection problem is accepted as adequate without further inferences concerning the necessity of the result of an act under all conditions of variation.

Other workers on problem solving and thinking have concerned themselves rather less with assumptions about content and its levels of inference and more with contributory mechanisms. Thus Luria's preoccupation with the retarded led him to emphasize the interdependence of functions one upon another, such as thinking on speech for example. Whilst in other respects adopting a point of view similar to Piaget's, the chief difference between the two would appear to be Luria's insistence on the importance of language in the thinking of defectives and young children. Piaget regards the level of thinking as not corresponding closely at each stage to the growth of language. Luria follows Pavlov, stressing the importance of secondary signals and tends to stress the dependence of stages of growth on social conditions rather than on levels of development. This introduces a difference in emphasis between the two theories.

Both Bruner (1957) and Bartlett (1958) study adults' thinking processes but Bruner, in so far as he is concerned with categorizing behaviour and its relationship with speech, touches on a problem which also concerns children and, of course, imbeciles. Each of these workers is concerned naturally enough with the growth and use of concepts. It is obviously out of a discussion of concept growth that modern discussions of thinking and symbolic learning emerged. Concept formation in children, through abstraction and generalization has been widely studied. Some of this work has been summarized by Vinacke (1952).

The nature of Bruner's observations represents a slightly different approach to thinking, but in making use of the idea of categorizing, he draws attention to two important notions, recognition of similarity and recognition of difference. Such recognition is in some respects basic to the thinking process at the mental level with which we are concerned. This kind of categorizing is said by Bruner to be involved in Piaget's notion of conservation. Although it may be the case that the recognition of perceptual similarity is somewhat different from the recognition of conceptual similarity, in one way or other recognition of identity is basic to both learning and thinking. Bruner makes some point of discussing categories both verbal and pre-verbal or perceptual and conceptual. He regards perceptual and conceptual categorizing as qualitatively identical. We are also interested in their use in relation to words or as wordless generalizations. The relationship between pre-verbal categorization and verbalization of similarity and difference obviously represents a very relevant problem for the study of imbecile learning. The nature of the relationship between language and thinking is a subject with which both Bruner and Luria are concerned and which has an extensive history starting from the viewpoint that thought has sometimes been considered to be sub-vocal language.

The relationship between signs and the things they signalize, e.g. a red spotted beak and feeding time, is one kind of relationship which has interested ethologists. They have attempted to maximize the significance of the sign itself or to maximize the reaction it evokes. Another kind of sign reaction, that of words and symbols signifying things and events, may be the basis of the categorizing which takes place in learning and which serves thinking. It is obviously a reversible transitive process, and both classifying into a category which may follow perception, or exemplifying from a category generally needs the aid of words. With humans of low intelligence both such processes require investigation. The criteria of categorization can be unitary or as more frequently happens, multiple. The recognition of, or searching for, the essential sign or signs may represent a matter for a casual glance or the necessity for a careful review of a number of items related in a certain way.

The multiple possibilities of error in categorizing, classifying, recognizing similarity, relating speech and primary signals, remembering appropriate rules and ignoring irrelevancies make directed thinking arduous if not unusual for literate adults. This skill, if skill it is, is practised over a limited subject range by a few people. Its skilled use depends on learning and it is naturally infrequent among imbeciles.

One process which has been mentioned by some of the experimenters referred to is that of classification. Another is that of coding. Bruner (1957) frequently uses these words in the same

B

sense. We don't. We will reserve the term coding for all these cognitive functions or processes which involve translation from one percept, sign or symbol to another percept, sign or symbol without change of meaning. We use classification to mean class inclusion whether inductive or deductive. Classification therefore includes the recognition of similarities and the discrimination of differences between stimuli.

However, the question remains somewhat obscure. Leonard (1955) using information theory concepts in discussing factors which influence channel capacity, takes into account ease of coding as an aid in the discrimination of stimuli. Deinninger and Fitts (1955) in the same volume, and elsewhere Fitts and Seeger (1953) and Fitts and Deinninger (1954) have discussed the ease of coding of displays under the heading of stimulus response compatibility. One of Leonard's conclusions from Crossman's (1955) work is that more bits of information can be readily coded under conditions of stimulus response compatibility than a lesser number of bits where there exists some degree of stimulus response incompatibility. He seems to hold that both discriminability and compatibility are relevant considerations in the assessment of ease of coding.

It also appears that the function of coding itself is subject to re-analysis as dependent on at least two other functions, discriminability and compatibility. Whatever their constituents we consider coding and classification may be part of the process of abstraction which for so long has been regarded as lacking in defectives.

The problem of choice complexity enters also into the assessment of a display. Learning takes place as Attneave (1954) has indicated according to the redundancy (repetition) present in any field. The same is naturally true of verbal sequences, and inferences due to redundancy may occur during a process of inspection. It seems reasonable to assume that if for example a defective's disabilities are concentrated in some weakness of inference, the same degree of redundancy would be less helpful to him than to someone of greater skill. The automatic use of redundancy, such for example as noticing that the two sides of a jar are the same, may be "given" to normals whereas to defectives it might be a construct. In such circumstances presumably a re-organization of displays would be indicated. In conditions indicating faulty inference a change of display might be needed to stress relevant aspects. A question arises therefore whether or not defectives make use of information with the same facility as normals? This question needs more precise formulation but it is a prototype of the kind of question we consider basic to the analysis of deficit. It needs qualification in so far as we must ask the question separately of all sub-diagnostic groups of defectives.

Firstly it might be the case that basic perceptual processes might be affected which as in birds or fish form the basis of imprinting. We have only scanty evidence that imprinting occurs in humans, none being reliable. Secondly we might find that children lacking visual or auditory experience might be deficient in orienting activities or might look for different groups of stimuli. In other words attentional as distinct from perceptual anomalies might arise. Recently Piaget (1961) discussed the effect of the focusing or fixating (centring) of attention or vision on the sampling of information from a perceptual field. In perceptual activities the act of comparing is a constant component. It seems likely that subnormals persist in fixating isolated aspects of a display, as distinct from normals who sample more widely.

The investigation of subnormality and faulty development due to neurological anomalies is by no means well developed and provides rather an inadequate set of hypotheses. However, in this field the strategy of psychological research must take account of any possible hyper-excitability or inertia of signalling systems even whilst trying to develop an overall plan of psychological description of functions. Distinct clinical groups may suffer from one characteristic difficulty whether perceptual, attentional, mnemonic or associative. This particular difficulty could be experimentally isolated in each subgroup of defectives by a planned research. For example, psychological tests to predict localization of damage are now used in predetermining major areas of cortical malformation in, for example, imbeciles. McFie's (1961) and Zangwill's (1960) studies suggest the possibility of crude but testable predictions which could be checked against major sub-diagnoses.

As a result of a research plan of this kind errors of learning and thinking could be analysed and compensated for or corrected where possible. In addition such an analysis could be tied to pre-dominant neuro-dynamic peculiarities as measurable in other ways. It is possible that subgroups of defect would reveal both physical and behavioural peculiarities which could be correlated and which might suggest further research.

Following this scheme the remaining chapters are concerned with particular aspects of learning and thinking processes in mental defectives or with presumably associated states of excita-bility. They follow the hierarchical pattern discussed above which may also be a generic one, that is they proceed from relatively given perceptual functions to relatively "constructed" operations which presumably must be learned.

Throughout the material is presented from the point of view of problems considered as part of general psychology. However, there is no doubt that any studies such as these must have re-education in mind and the experiments have the long term aim of increasing the potentials of defectives of imbecile grade. Such an educational process might include the communication between people which depends on the use of symbols and which is the substratum of thinking whether these symbols be spoken or written words, notes in a musical score, algebraic symbols or morse code. Obviously speaking and reading are likely to be the areas of activity in which guided instruction of imbeciles would prove most useful and it is with these two practical activities that one or two of the final experiments are concerned.

Thinking and learning are often considered to be closely linked and, whether this is so or not, the problems associated with learning and thinking draw often enough on similar sub-processes, famil-iarity with language, attention span, recognition of similarity, memory function and categorization skill. We have mentioned recent studies of thinking and problem solving in this chapter but we will inevitably be just as much concerned with learning and recall in the next and in subsequent experimental chapters.

There is an apparent difference, however, between some types of learning similar to conditioning and others which involve in-duction or concept development. Just as with thinking, there is a difference between association and an attempt to solve a problem by eliciting its structures or rules. In fact put in this way the close association between learning and thinking becomes apparent.

Learning of a cognitive kind as distinct from simple "sign-association" is often considered to be thinking. We will be interested in subsequent chapters in both rule deduction among imbeciles and to some extent in their conditionability, though the conditioning of motor skills has been investigated in many studies. We are therefore more concerned with processes such as those listed above which we consider relevant to what is sometimes called abstraction. This will include processes such as concept formation, induction and the formulation of rules or the delineation of classes, either for example in a simple case by the correct use of a descriptive noun or adjective, or in a more complex case by the formulation of such a rule as "x is always, or never, y".

In this first chapter the suggestion is made that the concepts of the I.Q. and psychometrics have retarded the study of the strategies and mechanism involved in thinking and problem solving. The chapter draws attention to the work of those who have in fact studied such strategies and mechanisms in children and adults. A preliminary analysis of processes involved in thinking and learning is suggested in terms of such operations as classification, transfer, verbalization, perception, discrimination, inference, memory and comprehension. Cognitive deficit must be estimated in terms of these processes. Further efforts should be made, however crudely, to link such findings with the known neuropathology of clinical sub-groups of severe mental defect.

CHAPTER II

LEARNING AND PROBLEM SOLVING IN THE SEVERELY SUBNORMAL

THE beginning of a more dynamic approach to problems of learning and thinking among imbeciles follows a period of recession in research of an educational kind. During this period the former approach to education, optimistic and experimental, gave place to a systematic categorizing by I.Q.

The analysis of cognition among defectives beginning with the systematic efforts of Itard (1801) to condition the behaviour of the "Wild boy of Aveyron" and proceeding via Seguin's (1846) educational probes, received what amounts to a shock apparently delivered by Binet. However Binet and Simon (1914) believed in the possibilities of educating the backward but believed also that this could be done only by scientific investigations. Kirk (1960) recently quoted Binet in a similar sense and went on to note that he had initiated an educational programme. Few of Binet's successors adopted such a view however.

Thus we are faced with a hiatus in the education of the mentally defective during the period after Binet's death until the 1940s. Evidence of training in this period is hard to come by although in the Mental Deficiency Colonies in England training schemes existed; but their scope was limited to craft training. It is clear from a reading of past issues of the *American Journal of Mental Deficiency* that educational programmes in the United States were uncommon in this period, i.e. from 1910 to 1940.

The beginning of the analysis of the functional aspects of learning began outside the area of mental deficiency. Such an analysis as that of Johnson (1955) is of primary interest because it begins to make a departure from the type of vector analysis which characterized the period of the measurement of intelligence and the development of tests. P. E. Vernon (1950) has summarized the growth of such factor theories from 1900 and there is no need to show how dominant has been their role in the study of academic performance. The normal English school system is based on the apparent implications of general factor theory as outlined by Burt (1926) in his appendix to the Hadow Report. However, the implications of the factor analysis of human abilities are still in dispute. The three main contending hypotheses, Thurstone's (1943) group factors, Spearman's (1927) general factor theory and Thomson's (1939) theory of neural bonds remain as plausible hypotheses and have had in practice a considerable effect. More recently, however, they have given ground to a different approach. This has happened not so much because they lack rigour or predictive value but because each one is associated with certain assumptions about the nature of intelligence which are no longer widely accepted. These assumptions are in fact not logically implied by, but simply associated with them, historically. Thus until recently it was assumed that measured intelligence was constant. Nothing in anyone of the theories mentioned involves this assumption, but their proponents tended to take this view working as they were in a period when genetic and eugenic opinions were dominant in England and America. This aspect of the theories gave them their fiat-like quality so that no test based on them ever led to an analytic or developmental approach to the qualities measured, until certain Iowa child development studies such as those of Skeels (1938) gave rise to a question in the minds of psychologists concerning the "given" quality of abilities.

The re-appraisal of some applied genetic theory combined with sociological studies tending to show the effect of experience on education and on intellectual skill, generated a new viewpoint. Excessively confident claims for the static nature of intelligence were dropped and psychologists commenced the study of problem solving and the circumstances favouring successful and unsuccessful thinking. In this period the development of knowledge about inductive logic played a part. Stebbing (1948) and Thouless (1953) drew attention not only to errors in reasoning but to varieties in modes of thought. Aristotle, Aquinas and Mediaeval logic, the basis of Spearman's nosology, were seen to present examples of only one kind of thinking.

It is in the light of this kind of theoretical development that the psychological re-analysis of problem solving capacity and thinking can have profound and direct effect on the study of severe subnormality. Both the new psychological interest in problem solving and the approach to severe subnormality partake of a common orientation which is perhaps best symbolized by Hebb's (1949) phase sequence theory of learning with its stochastic model of learning processes.

Much of the earlier work on problem solving by the mentally subnormal which is not extensive, reports accidental findings and is largely empirical in its conception. Most of it was carried out during the period of the primacy of the "abilities" theory of mental functioning.

Characteristic of the past history of the education of imbeciles has been that theory which informs the work of Itard (1801), Seguin (1846), Descoeudres (1928) and Montessori (1912). This is an approach to cognition which is characterized usually as a form of sense training. The interest of such an approach for those studying the severely subnormal arises with certain noted deficiencies which they were thought to show at a sensory level. Thus, for example, Birch and Mathews (1951) among others have demonstrated poor auditory discrimination in many defectives for tones above 6KC and O'Connor (1957) has shown a higher prevalence of colour blindness in imbecile males. Binet and Simon (1914) remarked on the incapacity of certain defectives to discriminate points on the skin and incorporated this test in their early measures of intelligence. There might thus be some grounds for carrying out investigations of sensory acuity before differentiation is tested at a higher level. Concept growth depends in part on the abstraction of common elements in percepts. If perception is impaired much else in the conceptual hierarchy must be at fault. This will not of course lead right back to Seguin or Montessori but will help to fill in an important gap in our knowledge of mental function.

The relative deficiency of verbal or non-verbal intelligence in those subnormals with I.Q. above 50 is another point which was noticed quite early on by such workers as Alexander (1935) and later by educators like Duncan (1942). It was the opinion of most investigators that two types of defectives could be differentiated, the verbal-above-performance and the performance-above-verbal groups. The latter was usually supposed to consist of familial defectives, the former of those who had been normal for some years and had contracted a disease such as encephalitis or had suffered cortical injury. The whole problem of verbal and non-verbal intelligence is still in need of further exploration. Mein and O'Connor (1960) have shown that the fact that defectives cannot give the meaning of any particular word indicates something more than that they do not know its meaning. It means often enough that they do not know the word nor use it in their ordinary speech.

Tizard (1960) has suggested that the limited potentials of severely subnormal children might be more fully developed if they were treated according to their mental ages. In his study 16 children aged 4½ to 10 with mental ages of between 1½ and 3½ were placed in a small residential unit run on nursery lines. These children made more progress in their social and emotional development than a control group in a large institution. Lyle's (1959) findings of the role of the social environment on verbal development was confirmed in this study. Previously he had shown that the language skills of imbecile children living at home were superior to those of comparable children in hospital. In connection with Tizard's experiment Lyle (1960) established that increases in verbal mental age were significantly greater for children in the nursery unit than for their controls in the institution. No differences between the groups were found in the level of non-verbal intelligence.

TABLE 1. DIFFERENTIAL EFFECTS OF BACKWARDNESS

Reasoning	
Long-distance mechanical memory	
Short-distance logical memory	(mental)
Short-distance mechanical memory	ratios below 85
Long-distance logical memory	
Duration of attention	
Speed of association	
Scope of attention	(mental)
Auditory perception	ratios above 85
Visual perception	

Of course verbal deficiencies are not the only ones which affect cognitive performance; Burt's (1937) analysis of such deficiencies among the E.S.N. is of interest. Burt's table is given here for both normals and backward children but more by way of illustrating the variety of mental processes than for comparison of the two groups. It re-introduced a detailed analysis of differential deficit which had been begun by Itard and Seguin.

There are clearly a number of ways in which a functional analysis of thought deficits might have proceeded but before attempting to illustrate our own preferred line of approach it seems desirable to assess more recent and current work in the cognitive processes of imbeciles. This is done with special reference to the manipulation of symbols and the operation of such mental processes as transfer. Three recent reviews have dealt with the available literature, McPherson (1947, 1958) and O'Connor (1958).

One of the earliest problem solving experiments with defectives was that of Ordahl and Ordahl (1915). Using a task which was a forerunner of a 5-choice apparatus, they found a relationship between success on this task and mental age. Most other investigators make the same comment but Woodrow (1946) for example objects to the identification of learning capacity and I.Q. and a number of studies such as those of Gordon, O'Connor and Tizard (1954), Tizard and Loos (1954) and McCulloch, Reswick and Roy (1955) showed characteristic lack of relationship between starting score and slope of learning curve or ultimate level reached. These investigations demonstrated the kind of inequality of skill which exists within a group of defectives of about the same I.Q. and furthermore showed the change which training can bring about and which is often ignored. Similar extensive studies of performance increments and their correlates showed the importance of incentives, and in the work of Claridge and O'Connor (1957) and O'Connor and Claridge (1958) the role of personality in learning among imbeciles. The importance of incentives was, of course, well demonstrated by Kuhlmann as early as 1904 and also by Gardner (1945).

The kind of problem solving experiment which in general has served the psychologist in mental deficiency up to 1948 was similar to that used in comparative psychology, since Thorndike (1911) developed its prototype. In this a reward is hidden and the subject is required to explore and manipulate the environment to obtain it. Sometimes the solution is inferable from cues and sometimes more simply from direct observation. It usually involves a speed factor only as a practical time limit, and it requires for the most part little motor dexterity. In this respect it corresponds with the scholastic tasks which were eventually emphasized in intelligence testing procedure succeeding Binet's, Simon's and Vaney's (1907) original design of motor, academic and physiological tests. Such investigations as those originally mentioned by McPherson (1947) include studies purporting to examine the use of principles in the solution of problems. Whiteside's (1934) experiment involved the verbalization of a principle of solution in the selection of geometrical figures. This was obviously a more complex task than the simple development of a principle of solution. Both this investigation and one by Gardner (1945) show a relationship with increasing mental age which is none the less loose enough to allow much variation. In addition, however, and in many respects it would seem to us more importantly, they both show the presence of a fairly good capacity for generalization from one task to another. This occurs despite what appears to be in Whiteside's study at least, a poor capacity to verbalize the principle of solution involved in the problem. Since 1948 the number of experiments devoted to abstract learning among subnormals of imbecile grade has increased. Stevenson and Iscoe (1955) on transposition and McCulloch, Reswick and Roy (1955) on word learning are relevant. Annett's (1957) study of defectives as poor information channels is also important. Other interesting investigations which should be mentioned are those of Barnett and Cantor (1957), Luria and Vinogradova (1959), Luria (1961), Griffiths, Spitz and Lipman (1959), Berkson and Cantor (1960), House and Zeaman (1958, 1959,a, b, and 1960,a, b), Stevenson and Ziegler (1957), Iscoe and Giller (1959), Cantor and Hottel (1955), Woodward (1959), Plenderleith (1956), Barnett, Ellis and Pryer (1960,a, b), Ellis, Pryer and Barnett (1959), Pascal, Stolurow, Zabarenko and Chambers (1951) Sloan and Berg (1957), Clarke and Blakemore (1961) and Clarke and Cookson (1962).

Kirk and McCarthy (1961) present a very interesting approach to the problem of language impairment. A battery of nine different tests is used, all concerned with language behaviour, through which a profile of psycho-linguistic functions is obtained. Kirk's theoretical model based on Osgood, Suci and Tannenbaum's theories, reflects modes of input and output, levels of organization and psycho-linguistic processes. Modes of input and output refer to visual and auditory stimuli and vocal and motor responses. Levels of organization include sequential, structural and semantic aspects of language, while decoding, association and encoding are aspects of the psycho-linguistic process. According to Kirk the test serves as a diagnostic tool, leading to a programme of remedial treatment which will utilize the child's assets to develop his area of deficiency.

Not all of these experiments nor a number of others which have appeared in unpublished reports and theses in the U.S.A. are concerned precisely with thinking or abstraction but most of them are concerned with what Russians tend to call higher nervous activity. Sometimes they attempt to correlate higher nervous activity with presumably more basic measures, such as reaction time, as in the study by Ellis and Sloan (1957) and Distifano, Ellis and Sloan (1958), or psychogalvanic response as in those of O'Connor and Venables (1956) and Collman (1959). However, a number are concerned directly with perceptual and conceptual problems at a relatively complex level, and in so far as we consider only these investigations they may be said to fall into several categories. Some are concerned with the detection of a principle of solution in a problem solving task, but more with the transfer of a principle which has been learned. Some are concerned with the verbalization of solutions of problems and others with the association of words and thinking. Some few are concerned solely with word learning and many more, not already referred to, with perceptual problems of various clinical categories of subnormals. Many of the latter are with brain injured subjects, frequently using Bender's Gestalt tests or Goldstein and Scheerer cubes or Strauss and Lehtinen's (1947) figure-ground tests. One experiment of this kind which will be discussed in detail later is a very interesting study by Gordon (1944) concerned with the discrimination of texture, brightness, chroma and form by sight and by touch.

Dealing firstly with some of the studies of concepts and of principles of solution, the experiments of Stevenson and Iscoe (1955) on transposition and Barnett and Cantor (1957) on the training of discrimination set are of interest. Stevenson and Iscoe compared the discrimination between squares of two sizes for pre-verbal defectives. They showed slower learning for defectives of M.A. 7·8 years compared with a matched normal group but transposition was observed in early trials. Barnett and Cantor used male defectives in a pre-training task. Half the subjects, all of whom had failed on a discrimination between upright and inverted triangles, were pre-trained on a "similar" task with semicircles, one a white semicircle on a black ground and the other a black semicircle on a white ground. The pre-trained group as distinct from the controls who did not have a relevant pre-training, "transferred" to the subsequent discrimination between upright and inverted triangles. Analysis of variance showed this difference to be relatively independent of mental age. The experiment is slightly complicated because in "set" training the experimental group learned to say aloud the two names "black" and "white" for the semicircles. This may have had a facilitating effect as can be seen from work such as that of House and Zeaman (1960,a) and Ellis, Barnett and Pryer (1959). Clarke and Blakemore (1961) and Clarke and Cookson (1962) have found that children of about I.Q. 40 show more transfer of training on sorting tasks than older patients of the same I.Q. They think that three separate though interacting processes contribute to this transfer: the building up of learning sets, i.e. "learning to learn", improved perceptual discrimination and improved conceptual discrimination. They also found that after a year without practice adolescent imbeciles were able to carry out sorting tasks very much better than at the initial learning sessions. These studies, which are representative of some others, seem to indicate the possibility of the relative intactness of transfer abilities among imbeciles. Transfer from one level of difficulty to another has been discussed by House and Zeaman (1960,a) and Russian authors such as Liublinskaya (1955) have also dealt with training problems in terms of preparatory set. House, Zeaman, Orlando and Fischer (1957) showed that three-dimensional discriminations are learned more easily by defectives than are two-dimensional discriminations. They inferred from this that transfer from easy to hard discrimination found with rats to be more marked than from hard to hard, would also be more marked with defectives. Three groups were used in a study by House and Zeaman

(1960), one trained on patterns only, one on objects similar to the pattern stimuli to which they were transferred and one on objects dissimilar from the subsequent patterns. Objects were vertically mounted 14 in. masonite forms of either a T and a square or a cross and a circle. Their pattern equivalents were of the same size and painted on wedges. Colours were the same. Results showed that both forms of object training aided pattern discrimination, and similarity of object and pattern was superior to dissimilarity. After some discussion House and Zeaman conclude that discrimination of pattern is aided through the exposure of the subject to a relevant cue in pre-training.

In discussing this problem House and Zeaman have touched on an issue which we think is of significance for the main point of discussion in this book. The mental operation of translating the perception of objects into the perception of patterns is part at least of an overall type of mental function which we wish to consider in a number of its manifold forms. In House and Zeaman's discussion the translation function is complicated by perceptual questions and in all probability this kind of transfer always will involve perceptual as well as conceptual patterns. To resolve the contributions made by each separate function would require the resolution of the problems which Hume and Kant presented severally and from different viewpoints. We do not think it likely that this problem will be resolved by our experiments, but we assume that mental deficiency presents us with conditions of poor development which, by diminishing or arresting the rate of mental growth at relatively early levels, enables us to analyse historically the growth of concepts and perceptual skills. In this respect only, experiments may help us to throw new light on this ancient epistemological question.

Another group of recent studies which have raised considerable interest in Europe although they have not been widely known until recently in the U.S.A. are those from the Institute of Defectology in Moscow. Many of these have been conducted in association with Luria and are referred to in his London Lectures (1961). Much of this research in common with other work from Moscow and Leningrad has been concerned with functions involving language. Luria has stated his views on language in various articles and a small book, all recently published in English (1958, 1959,a,

1959,b, 1959,c). In all this work Luria acknowledges the original suggestions of Vigotsky (1939) who pointed out the formative function of adult speech in the development of a child's mental processes. Words have in fact a directive function from adult to child and at first remain directive only so long as they are spoken by the adult. However, Luria conceives of this directive process gradually becoming internalized. This proceeds by stages and some functions are internalized before others. So impelling or activating signals, comments or words become internalized before inhibitory ones. As the critical age for the internalization of the inhibitory function of words seems to be around the age of 5 years, this set of findings has considerable relevance for the study of the problem solving behaviour of imbeciles and for their thinking processes. One of the techniques developed by Luria and Vinogradova (1959) was modelled on a study by Schwarz (1948). Plethysmographic records of finger volume or the volume of other blood vessels or both are recorded. Conditioned reflexes are then established to words. After this the generalization of these reflexes are classified according to whether such generalizations have followed a phonic or semantic pattern. According to Luria and his colleagues such generalizations show a phonic pattern in imbeciles but a semantic one in normals. Thus responses generated by the stimulus "doctor" generalize to "dictor" instead of to "physician". Lacey and Smith's (1954) work reinforces this conclusion as far as normals are concerned but Luria and Vinogradova have raised a question of the development of vocabularies and what they call "elective generalization" in defectives which needs to be examined. Likewise Luria's (1959,a) work on the responses of imbeciles to verbal signals raises the question of whether or not they can respond selectively to a general instruction. It is also questionable, following his work, whether imbeciles may be thought to be able to respond to "inhibitory" stimuli even when reinforced differentially at each stage of conditioning. Most stimuli, whether signalling a positive or a negative response, elicit a positive one from imbeciles.

Luria (1958) also makes the point that most of the processes which we regard as typical of higher nervous function, such as complex perception, intelligent memorization, voluntary attention and logical thinking were thought by Vigotsky to be formed in the course of the child's interaction with his social environment. As such a view is commonly held by Russian psychologists, we would be able to regard Luria as similar to Hebb in having espoused a theory of the development of mental processes in which each stage is dependent on previous stages. The development of selective attention is demonstrated by Luria who remarks that the growth of active memorization, voluntary action and abstract thinking have each been shown to be strongly influenced by the selective, emphatic and reinforcing quality of adult speech. In fact the similarity of Inhelder's and Piaget's (1958), Hebb's (1949) and the Russian view can be recognized in the following quotation from Luria (1958): "Indeed, the formation of complex mental activity always required strict consistency and succession of individual operations: sometimes, if only a single link of training is missed, if a certain stage in the development of the necessary operation is not properly worked up, the entire process of further development becomes retarded, and the formation of higher mental functions assumes an abnormal character."

For our present purposes the Russian work, emphasizing as it does the importance of the role of speech and language and the significance of inhibition in both the formation of concepts and selective voluntary behaviour, throws up another aspect of thought processes which is relevant for our study of the learning and thinking of imbeciles. In so far as the failure to develop speech and hence concepts impedes problem solving, Luria's statements can be tested. So also can the interference of immediate stimuli with general instructions as outlined in this work. One must keep in mind the deaf-mute who without the benefit of speech none the less has a complex system of sign language, thoughts and concepts.

Zaporozhets' (1955) work should be mentioned because although not directly connected with words and their influence on perception and thought, it is concerned with the dominance of receptors. In some respects this question is similar to that referred to by Luria concerning verbal facility. In the case of the experiment discussed above the first signalling system in all senses was thought to be dominant in defectives—so that association in an auditory modality proceeded by phonic rather than by semantic similarity. If we consider the situation of two senses competing instead of primary and secondary signalling systems, we see that a similar problem arises. Luria points out that at the age of 1 year 4 months to 1 year 6 months children formerly trained to find a reward under the left of two cups will make a move to choose the left cup when they have just seen the experimenter put the reward under that on the right. A delay of 10 seconds may serve to force the child to reflect on the visual trace and choose according to vision rather than motor habit. Luria's report of this experiment makes it clear that the dominance of motor movement at this stage is only overcome with some difficulty by competing visual cues.

This is one instance of a kind of transfer process described by House and Zeaman's (1960,a) work on perceptual transfer from three to two dimensions. In both cases, a problem of compatibility is raised, the problem in one case involving a translation, in the other involving a recognition of a difficulty in, or a barrier to, translation. In the first instance translation takes place in a situation where compatibility of response to different though similar stimuli is to be encouraged. In the second case a new response is enjoined by a new stimulus and the translation of an old remembered set of stimuli into the new environment is contra-indicated. But the incompatability of the previous response must be learned; nothing but experience can indicate the prior importance in this instance of the visual cue.

However, taking account of child development stages there is a further complication in Luria's reported experiment. This is the fact that experience may come first by touch and later by sound and by sight. There may, therefore, be a hierarchy of development through which the child must go, as Luria's experiment suggests. If this is indeed the case, not only are we faced with translations between the first and second signal systems but between modalities within the first system. Such transfers must be made developmentally in time, as well as from one signal system to another at any one instant. Alternatively it may be supposed that the integration of information from different modalities is essential for object identification. Imbeciles may be deficient in this integrating activity.

Such experiments and more especially an entirely different group from Leningrad, those of Ananiev's (1961), Zinchenko and Lomov (1960) and their colleagues, reveal the importance of the

c

isolation of the essential signal qualities of an object. The signal-izing aspect of percepts is dealt with in a provocative manner by Mescheriakov (1953) in discussing the formation of image devel-opment in a blind deaf mute child. In summarizing the child's experience he says: "As a result of repeated manipulations with objects, a signal perception develops, i.e. the total image of an object is actualized from a single feature perceived."

This quality of reduction of many stimuli into a signal stimulus is an important aspect of the orienting activity of humans and animals which we need to take into account in studying processes involved in learning and thinking. The selection and emphasis of significant cues is of importance in perception. It is also obviously highly relevant to the determination of what is to be the represen-tative quality of an object or event and the manner in which it is to be translated into a sign, or image, or a symbol. In some respects this process involves translation problems which have something in common with those we have already mentioned above.

Transfer processes of this kind in perception bring us very close to some observations made by Leonard (personal communi-cation) with defectives. He noticed that connections obvious to us were by no means obvious to imbeciles. Thus the juxtaposition of a signal light and a button did not necessarily mean to an im-becile that a general instruction to "press when the light comes on" should be interpreted as pressing the button closest to the illu-minated bulb. Imbeciles may not have developed an understanding of the importance of spatial proximity and contact in mechanical causality. Piaget (1930) has shown this development in normal children.

The question of discrimination of colours and shapes has been raised in a study by House and Zeaman (1958) in which imbecile children learned a colour-form discrimination problem more slowly than did monkeys and normal children. They attribute this to a discrimination deficit. If additional qualities are added to the objects to be discriminated the task becomes easier. It might seem to be the case that discrimination of similar cues is difficult for defec-tives. Clearly when we take account of Leonard's observation and House and Zeaman's (1959,b) study, the perceptual structuring of a display might be rather different for normals on the one hand and defectives on the other. It is also clear that only the most tentative exploration of these differences has been made to date. It is apparent that such workers as House and Zeaman take the view that attentional questions are primary in the learning problems of imbeciles.

Since Binet *et. al.* (1907) observations, discrimination and recognition of similarities have been noted. This is essentially a form of analysis and synthesis, but some experimenters have suggested that visual perception of a discriminative kind must be conditioned. In this respect it would be a basic quantum in any thought process because the analysis and synthesizing processes would be based on the initial units of differentiation. These would be a function of both the physiology of the optic tract and experience based on the key or signal qualities of objects, for example whether they move or are stationary, whether they are green or red. More basic even than this perhaps is the question of whether or not they emerge from a background.

This reference to the failure of the emergence of basic visual patterns takes the process away from the usual "concrete-abstract" sub-division which has been the stock-in-trade of most workers in this field.

So far as these statements are concerned "abstraction" has been the most characteristic shortcoming of the thinking of mental defectives. The term is vague and we need to consider what it might mean. If, as some workers suggest, perceptual processes are deficient among imbeciles we may need to reconsider this classical sub-division. Obviously if perception is impaired, abstraction will suffer. This is true even if we must learn to perceive objects, as Hebb (1949) suggests. The deficiency therefore would be brought back nearer a basic level of learning and not removed from common perceptual problems.

At whatever level we might be faced with problems of equivalence and difference, such problems inevitably involve translation. It is in this process of translation and coding that we consider that many of the cognitive problems of imbeciles consist. It is, however, the purpose of the experiments reported below to consider this and other functions involved in learning and thinking and to suggest which is dominant as an explanation of cognitive incompetence.

This review of work on the cognitive problems of defectives

mostly of imbecile grade has brought out different trends. The need for sense training has been suggested, as perceptual impairment may be one of the reasons for the imbecile's failure to abstract. It has been shown that presentation of relevant cues in training facilitates sensory discrimination and the discrimination of patterns. It has been suggested that lack of perception of sensory patterns or basic Gestalten may explain the failure of imbeciles to reason and to solve problems.

Failure of imbeciles to develop adequate speech has been noted. It is not so much that they do not understand syntax, but that they do not know many words. Perhaps as a result their thinking is deficient, although we do not wish to suggest that it is the sole cause of their defect. The acquisition of and internalization of verbal self-direction, especially of an inhibitory kind, is also thought to be defective among the severely subnormal.

Cue selection and attention and the transfer of learned principles have been investigated. The latter would appear to be reasonably adequate in imbeciles, whereas the former would appear to be grossly deficient.

Whether it is the isolation by training and experience of a signalizing cue as representing a whole display, or the formulation of a motor act or a principle of solution as a verbal proposition, encoding and decoding of information will certainly be involved. Another tendency in the research reviewed is that of regarding processes as interlinked so that one may not take place without the full development of another. These principles and others will be developed in reporting our own work.

CHAPTER III

VISUAL PERCEPTION AND SEVERE SUBNORMALITY

SENSORY perception has always been considered basic to cognitive functioning. In the eighteenth century Pereire, Rousseau, and subsequently Itard, Guggenbühl and Seguin, were each impressed by the importance of sense training. Their theories were developed by successive schools in other countries and in later years, for example by Pestalozzi and Montessori. Itard (1801) believed that in the savage of Aveyron he had been dealing with a child deprived of normal sensory experience. He thought that the boy, Victor, might be made normal if such experience were artificially provided. Though disappointed with the limited success of his efforts, Itard nevertheless thought that Victor had been transformed in some respects.

Pereire's educational system was firmly based on the notion of the interdependence of the senses. He taught deaf mutes to speak through the perception of touch by training awareness of vibrations. This led to the formulation of a doctrine which we thought to be of interest because of some of our findings concerning intersensory functions.

The formulation most readily available from material published at that time is summarized by Seguin (1866):

"1st. That the senses, and each one in particular, can be submitted to physiological training by which their primordial capability may be indefinitely intellectualized.

"2nd. That one sense may be substituted for another as a means of comprehension and of intellectual culture.

"3rd. That the physiological exercise of a sense corroborates the action, as well as verifies the acquisitions of another.

"4th. That our most abstract ideas are comparisons and generalizations by the mind of what we have perceived through our senses.

25

"5th. That educating the modes of perception is to prepare pabulum for the mind proper.

"6th. That sensations are intellectual functions performed through external apparatus as much as reasoning, imagination, etc., through more internal organs."

Elsewhere, of course, Seguin (1846) had already developed his ideas of the use of physiological training in the treatment of idiots.

After Seguin's disquisition there is a long gap till Burt's (1937) analysis of the sensory deficits associated with backwardness. In his sample of London and Birmingham children he demonstrated that the association of both auditory and visual defect with mental subnormality was considerable. Burt always took the view that sensory impairment could not be solely responsible for subnormal intelligence, but other earlier and later writers, not excluding Tredgold (1952) and Binet and Simon (1914), were disposed to take another view. Birch and Mathews (1951) have confirmed Burt's findings but attempted no explanation of the results. However, precise data are scanty and few systematic investigations have followed Burt's. Despite brilliant work on normals and animals, such as that of Bexton, Heron and Scott (1954) and that of Hebb (1949), Harlow (1949) and Weinstein (1945) the perception of subnormals has been examined only cursorily. Lack of investigation in this field represents perhaps the biggest gap in the study of cognition in subnormals.

There are few reported anomalies which might point to a basic difference in the sensory equipment of severely subnormal patients. High frequency deafness, often regarded as a contributory cause for mental subnormality may or may not be connected with the sense organs. The authors know of no figures for the frequency of occurrence of this, and likewise no figures for the incidence of mental subnormality among the blind are available. O'Connor (1957) tested male imbeciles for Red-Green and Yellow-Blue forms of colour blindness. He found 13·3 per cent of his sample to show this anomaly. This is a significantly higher percentage than is usually found in normals, as for example in Pickford's (1951) study where 7·6 per cent of males were found to be colour blind.

Theories such as those of Goldstein and Scheerer (1941) and Strauss and his colleagues, which state that cortical lesions interfere with visual perception, should apply to imbeciles. Studies of brain damage may have shown this to be the case, for example those of Strauss and Lehtinen (1947) and Strauss and Kephart (1955), but subsequent work reviewed elsewhere by O'Connor (1958,b) has put the validity of such research in doubt.

Although it is reasonable to infer that the manifold lesions or malformations in the brain of severely subnormal patients interfere with integrating and connecting processes, the most remarkable feature about such patients is that gross developmental anomalies can occur in the cortex without any outstanding effect on the direct reflection of the external world through the senses. It is uncertain whether the frequently reported perceptual abnormalities, such as confusion of figure and ground, breakdown of Gestalt patterns, and rotations and reversals are a general characteristic of the perception of imbeciles or are due to the manner in which the task is presented and the response demanded.

Berkson (1960,I, II, III) reports an interesting series of experiments in which he attempts to analyse the factors which contribute to slowness in subnormals when compared with normal subjects on visual-motor reaction time tasks. His first experiment investigated the perceptual duration threshold of mentally deficient and normal boys. The length of time a stimulus has to be presented in a choice situation before it is correctly recognized, will be a limiting factor in RT, since a person does not respond to a stimulus until he identifies it. Berkson considered that I.Q. may be related to the duration threshold in such a way that people of lower intelligence need a longer presentation of a stimulus in order to identify it correctly. Consequently the duration of stimulus presentation was varied, using a tachistoscope and a modified method of minimal changes. The stimuli were circles containing a dot in one of four positions. The S's task was to report the location of the dot. No significant difference in duration threshold was found between normal and subnormal subjects.

It was considered that complexity of display rather than perceptual speed might result in increasing slowness in the reaction times of subnormals. Consequently in his next experiments Berkson compared groups of subnormals and normals on two pairs of visual RT tasks, varying in stimulus complexity or response complexity. In the task in which the number of signal lights was changed, but the required response kept the same, no interaction of I.Q. groups and task was observed. A significant interaction was obtained between I.Q. and tasks in which the stimulus was held constant and the complexity of the required response was varied. Berkson concluded from his results that they did not support the belief that I.Q. is related to the speed of visual information reception, but that it is related to functions involved in the speed of performance of response.

These experiments have been reported here in some detail because they seem to us to provide an example of an approach which has sought to analyse performance in simple tasks. They determined which specific functions were related to the constantly demonstrated positive relationship between speed and intelligence.

Although Annett (1957) has suggested that information load rather than perceptual or motor abilities determined reaction times in his subnormal subjects, in some groups of subnormals at least response mechanisms rather than the process of intake of information seem to be impaired. Cassel (1949) showed that faulty reproduction of designs by subnormals could not be attributed to perceptual impairment but was due to some other factor, such as lack of attention and memory or inability to initiate and carry out a motor response. We have carried out a series of studies which have some bearing on the relative impairment of input and output mechanisms. In assessing the capacity of imbeciles to follow general verbal instructions we (O'Connor and Hermelin 1961,a) had demonstrated that when obliged to do so they could transpose a stimulus from one sensory modality to another apparently through the medium of words. An example will make this clear. An instruction to recognize a previously seen picture by selecting its spoken name from other names was given to imbeciles of I.Q. 35 and aged 10–15 years. They succeeded better in this task than in another in which they saw pictures of objects and then were asked to distinguish them from other pictures, by sight. Several similar experiments confirmed this finding suggesting the success of "cross-modal" responses and also suggesting the importance of verbal coding in accounting for the superiority of such responses.

We now wished to ascertain whether or not the cross modality effects would disappear when words no longer facilitated coding

from one modality to another (Hermelin and O'Connor 1961,a)·
We therefore compared stereognostic discrimination and recognition among imbeciles with their visual discrimination and recognition, and of course, following the usual design of these experiments,
two other patterns of response. These were touch examination with
visual recognition and visual examination with tactile recognition.
Our hypothesis in this experiment was that cross-modal effects
were unlikely to be shown because fewer words of a simple kind
were available to describe complex abstract shapes. If this
were indeed so and we chose shapes which imbeciles would find
hard to name, then they would have difficulty in translating tactile
into visual sensations and the reverse. In this event the superiority
of cross-modal over uni-modal responses would be lost. We used
as shapes Greek and Russian letters cut out in hardboard. The
results seemed to confirm our expectations. We found in fact no
cross modality effects.

An accidental finding of the experiment was that we noted the
relative superiority of the tactile inspection-recognition procedure
in imbeciles. Compared with a normal control group, matched for
mental age, the imbeciles' visual scores were poor. If, however,
they explored and identified the stimuli stereognostically they did
better than the normal children.

This led us to compare the stereognosis of mongols and imbeciles
(O'Connor and Hermelin 1961,b). We repeated the study, this
time comparing normals, mongols and non-mongol imbeciles of
like chronological age, i.e. 15–25 years. We also included normal
children aged 5 years who were matched for mental age with the
subnormals. The procedure was as follows: each subject was
either presented successively with five shapes for visual inspection
or he had to feel its outline with his hands when it was behind a
screen and out of sight. Immediately after this, these five shapes
had to be identified from among five other, similar ones, again
either tactually or visually. We used only like modality procedures,
so that those presented with visual stimuli were given visual
recognition tests and those who had inspected the shapes with
their hands without seeing them had to recognize them stereognostically.

The data are the correct "Yes" and "No" responses to each of
a sequence of stimuli. A chance score is taken to be at the level

of 50 per cent correct answers. This may be achieved by giving uniformly positive or negative replies, or in the more expected way by a random distribution of "Yes" and "No" answers. A transformation suggested by A. E. Maxwell on the principle underlying Cox's (1958) method for the analysis of trends in binary sequences was adopted to give a measure for each subject of the deviation of his score from chance. The stimuli were ranked and a score was obtained as a sum of those ranks to which a correct response was given. This process was repeated ranking in the opposite direction and the ranks again summed. The mean of the two scores of correct rankings was taken as a final score which was expressed as a positive or negative deviation of the figure obtained from a chance distribution of success or failure (i.e. half the total sum of ranks).

The mean results of the stereognostic and visual recognition scores are given in the table.

TABLE 2. COMPARATIVE SCORES OF NORMALS AND IMBECILES
ON TACTILE AND VISUAL RECOGNITION

	N	Mean stereognostic recognition scores	Mean visual recognition scores
Normal children	12	$23·37 \pm 11·6$	$24·29 \pm 12·6$
Non-mongol imbecile adults	12	$28·87 \pm 7·2$	$19·25 \pm 10·3$
Normal adults	12	$28·87 \pm 7·8$	$34·37 \pm 4·4$
Mongol imbecile adults	12	$12·83 \pm 7·6$	$22·91 \pm 8·4$

If the performance of imbecile adults is compared with that of normal adults and normal children it appears that the subnormals are scarcely the equal of children in visual discrimination—a fact also noted by House and Zeaman (1960,b). However, they are the equal of adults in tactile discrimination. These same imbeciles are, from a perceptual point of view, imbeciles in visual but not in tactile recognition. We will discuss the implications of these results further on. Here we want to stress two points. One is that some imbeciles (non-mongols) are as good in stereognostic discrimination as normals of like chronological age. The development of their visual discrimination, however, is impaired or at any rate grossly retarded. Comparing normal adults with normal children on the present results, tends to confirm Hebb's (1949) view that the ability to identify complex visual shapes at a glance is not perfected in young children. Young children may rely as much on kinesthetic and tactile cues as on vision to explore their environment. In the growing normal, the visual and auditory senses gradually become the main sources of information about events in the outside world, while touch and kinesthetic sensitivity may develop little. However this may be, the experiment just described carefully separates visual and tactile stimuli and some imbeciles achieve a normal adult level in stereognosis. We would like to emphasize this finding because it appears to have implications for the education of imbecile children. Such implications concern both the relative strengths or abilities of stereognosis as opposed to vision—as we have shown, and conceivably their interaction also.

The second finding concerns the difference between mongol and non-mongoloid imbeciles. Mongols are inferior to non-mongols of the same I.Q. in tactual recognition. This may be accounted for by the small cerebellum, and the resulting hypotonia and poor organization of movement common in mongols. This suggestion needs further analysis. Lesions in areas 5 and 7 may also lead to stereognostic amnesia, according to Ruch, Fulton and German (1938).

In another study Hermelin and O'Connor (1961,b) sought to confirm these findings of differential abilities of mongols, non-mongol imbeciles and normals of like mental age in the motor response area and the absence of such differences in visual perception. We also wished to compare apperception of directional as compared with proportional cues in the designs. Halpin's (1955) findings suggested that the frequently reported rotation errors in subnormals could not be considered as a form of behaviour which could be predicted reliably from one visual-motor task to another. We also compared perception with short term memory for designs, but we will report this aspect of the experiment in its appropriate context.

Groups of 16 normal and of 16 mongol and non-mongol institutionalized subnormal patients each, took part in the experiment. The mean I.Q. of the patient groups was 36 points and the mean age 18 years. The normal children, aged between $4\frac{1}{2}$ and $5\frac{1}{2}$ were matched with the subnormal for mental age. Four directionally and four proportionally orientated line drawings of simple shapes were used. They were drawn in black on white cards $5\frac{1}{2}$ in. by $5\frac{1}{2}$ in. and are reproduced in the accompanying figures. Performance on four tasks was compared. These were (1) matching, (2) recognizing, (3) copying and (4) reproducing designs. In the matching tasks the cue figure was displayed and an identical one had to be selected from amongst three others, which differed from the correct one in orientation or proportion only. In the recognition trials the correct design had to be selected from amongst others from memory, after the prototype had been removed. In the drawing tests, (3) and (4) above, a stimulus figure had to be copied while displayed, or reproduced from memory after it had been removed from sight.

Each stimulus prototype was presented for 10 seconds and there was a 20–30 second interval between presentations. Each subject was presented in turn with all eight figures (i.e. four directional and four proportional ones) and was tested under any of the four conditions. Each design was presented for one trial only and the first response was scored. The assignment of a particular figure for a condition, and the order of conditions, was balanced according to a Graeco-Latin square design.

TABLE 3. TOTAL SCORES OUT OF AN OPTIMAL 28

	Matching		Recognition	
	Directional	Proportional	Directional	Proportional
Normal	20	28	16	18
Imbecile	20	19	16	14
Mongol	20	21	12	14

	Copying		Reproduction	
	Directional	Proportional	Directional	Proportional
Normal	22	20	21	22
Imbecile	24	19	19	21
Mongol	13	15	14	13

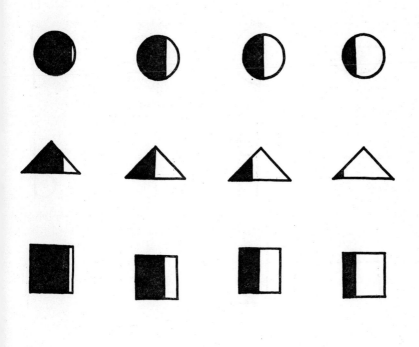

Fɪɢ. ɪ. Proportional figures.

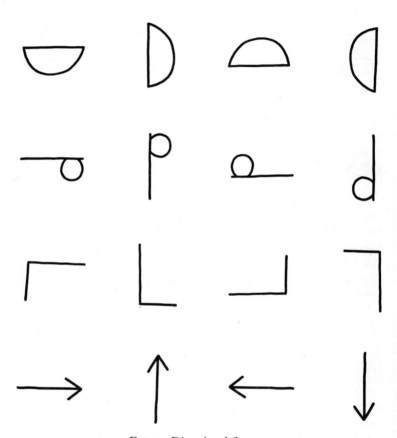

Fɪɢ. 2. Directional figures.

The total scores for each of the groups under each condition are given in the table. They represent number of correct responses out of an optimal 28. Two analyses of variance were carried out, one for conditions of matching and recognition and one for copying and reproducing the stimuli. The first analysis, using matching and recognition scores, showed no significant difference in performance of normals, mongols and non-mongols. There was also no significant difference in the ability to match and recognize directionally as distinct from proportionally oriented designs. Although normal scores on proportional matching and recognition seem different from those for the other two groups, the difference is not statistically significant. However, normals, mongols and non-mongols alike differed in their ability to match or recognize the stimuli, obtaining significantly lower scores ($P = 0.001$) in the recognition tasks. None of the interactions was significant.

The second analysis was concerned with scores obtained from the drawings. Each drawing was given a score of 2 if "apperception of Gestalt" as well as the critical directional or proportional cue were correctly reproduced. A score of 1 was given when only one of these two relevant features was present in the drawing. Drawings which showed neither of these two characteristics were scored as 0. Analysis of variance on the drawing scores did not result in a significant difference between conditions. Copying and reproducing designs from memory produced the same results. There was, however, a significant difference between the groups. While normals and non-mongoloid imbeciles obtained equal scores, those of the mongols were significantly lower.

Thus in this experiment, as in the previous one, comparison of normals, mongols and non-mongoloid imbeciles of like mental age on visual matching and recognition tasks did not result in a difference between the groups. The results did not support conclusions of visual and perceptual impairment in severely subnormal patients when compared with young normal children. Nor did they indicate that tendencies for reversal and rotation of designs were more marked in subnormals than in normals. On the other hand, the drawing tasks indicate that mongols have more difficulties than non-mongoloid imbeciles in reproducing a correctly perceived design.

The correct perception of similarities and differences may be a somewhat more complex operation than matching and recognition. We have carried out two experiments investigating this. The first was concerned with generalization from one member of a series of simple stimuli to neighbouring ones. The second involved discrimination of more complex shapes. Hebb (1958) points out that generalization between stimuli on a scale, differing in pitch, intensity, brightness or size, may be independent of learning and experience. The generalization is probably sensory and does not involve mediating processes. Pattern discrimination on the other hand seems to involve such mediating processes, which are built up by experience.

The first study investigated the degree to which normal and subnormal children generalized an established response to stimuli on scales of intensity, brightness or size. First the subjects were trained to discriminate between the two most distant points on a scale, for instance between the loudest and softest tone on a five-point intensity scale. After this the three intermediate stimulus values were presented repeatedly in random order. If a subject had been trained to respond to a soft and not to the loud tone he was asked to give a response if subsequent stimuli were "like" the previously positive, and "unlike" the negative stimulus.

In both groups generalization was most frequent to the adjacent and least frequent to the most distant scale position of the interpolated stimuli. However, as the table shows, the normals responded more frequently to the scale point next to the cue stimulus than did the subnormals. This greater specificity of the defectives may

TABLE 4. MEAN GENERALIZATION SCORES

Scale points	Imbecile score	Normal score
2	111	132
3	61	69
4	32	26

be a result of a more strongly reinforced initial discrimination response. The subnormals needed significantly more trials to learn the initial discrimination between distant points of the stimulus scales. Defectives usually take longer than normals in learning to identify any feature in their environment. Their specificness, which has often been observed and been equated with "concreteness" may well be a function of the initially large number of trials which they need in order to learn, although examination of individual records does not support this interpretation. However, even although subnormals tend to be specific in their responses, and are often unable to recognize similarities, they also find difficulty in recognizing essential differences. The question therefore arises whether displays can be presented in such a way that essential differences are emphasized and accidental similarities minimized.

A second point is whether, having initially learned that one dimension of a stimulus may vary, while others remained constant, the subjects would be able to recognize the relevant similarity in a variety of situations. Weinstein's (1945) experiments with Rhesus monkeys may be relevant in this connection. The monkeys were required to perform a sorting task, matching objects with either a triangle or an ellipse. Keeping one relationship, in this case colour, constant while varying other features such as shape and size of the object throughout a number of trials, he eventually trained the monkeys to utilize uncoloured shapes of a triangle and an ellipse as cues, according to which red and blue objects had to be sorted. Similarly, Harlow (1949) found that apes could build up learning sets which enabled them to single out common features in otherwise different objects.

One way of stressing differences between stimuli would be to multiply the dimensions in which they vary from each other. Miller (1956) showed that in normals the capacity to process information is increased by adding to the number of ways in which stimuli differ. With the method of absolute judgement, only up to seven values of an unidimensional stimulus variable can be discriminated. If, however, the stimuli differ from one another in several different ways, the number which can be identified without confusion is greatly increased. These findings may prove relevant in overcoming difficulties which subnormals often have in learning to discriminate between complex shapes such as printed or written letters and words. The following experiments therefore tested whether word recognition could be made easier

D

by adding additional distinguishing stimulus attributes. Imbeciles of below 40 I.Q. and aged between 9 and 15 were the subjects in the experiment. Twelve matched pairs of subjects were selected according to age and I.Q. and each member was randomly allocated to the experimental or the control group.

The material consisted of 24 white cards, 25×75 mm, on each of which a word was printed. There were four words: "Horse", "Swan", "Panda" and "Fish". Each word was printed in six different sizes of lettering. The size of the lettering is best described by the height of the letters. This was 3 mm for the smallest and 10 mm for the largest size. In the intermediate sizes the lettering measured 4, 5, 6 and 8 mm respectively. An example of the way in which each word was presented for learning in a five-stage procedure for the experimental group is illustrated.

A picture which represented the cue word was shown to the child and he was asked to name the picture. Then he was asked to select the printed word which he thought was the equivalent name from the other three words. The cue word was presented in 10 mm letters and the lettering for other words was 3 mm. If the subject chose correctly he was given a reward, if not he was told which printed word was the correct one. Each trial stage was repeated until 10 consecutive responses were obtained. The position of the correct word in relation to the others was of course varied in a predetermined way from trial to trial. After the criterion had been reached the next stage followed immediately without comment. Thus in successive trials the size of the cue word was gradually reduced, until the height of the letters was equal to that of the other words, i.e. 3 mm. On the following days the same procedure was followed with the remaining words, until all had been learned in this manner. Following this, a memory test was given. This consisted of one 1-trial session in which the four words, all printed the same size, were given to the child and he was asked to read them out, and match them with the appropriate pictures. The control group went through the same series of trials except that all words were presented throughout at the same lettering height, i.e. 3 mm.

At the first trial stage the experimental group needed a mean of 2·9 trials to learn to criterion compared with a mean of 10·5 trials for the controls. Subsequent stages led to one trial learning in the

panda   horse   fish   swan

swan   fish   panda   horse

horse   swan   panda   fish

panda   fish   horse   swan

swan   horse   fish   panda

fish   panda   swan   horse

FIG. 3. Arrangement of words for reading experiment.

experimental subjects. The control group also improved significantly in the number of trials needed to relearn. However, taking learning as a whole, the subjects in the experimental groups needed a mean of 7·8 presentations to learn any cue word, while the controls needed 19·3 trials. This difference is statistically highly significant.

No significant difference between the groups was found in the retention tests. The experimental subjects read 3 out of the 4 words correctly while the control subjects obtained a score of 2·3. This result will be discussed in its appropriate context, together with other material on the memory of defectives. As far as economy of learning effort is concerned it may be concluded that multi-dimensional variation between stimuli not only facilitates differentiation between them through stressing differences, but that keeping one stimulus feature constant while varying others helps to single out such common features in different stimuli and situations. Such variation stabilizes the subject's set to recognize differences as well as similarities.

Similar findings are reported by House and Zeaman (1960,a), who found that initial presentation of three-dimensional stimuli facilitated subsequent two-dimensional discrimination. However, they conclude from their series of experiments that at a mental age level of 5 years normals with their higher I.Q.s are significantly better in discrimination learning than defectives. They suggest that the ability to name the positive and negative cues may be related to the ease of visual discrimination. They also found that the introduction of novel stimuli either positive or negative can facilitate discrimination learning.

Some of the findings reported here can be adduced as evidence to support our main contention that the gross developmental anomalies present in the severely subnormal yet leave elementary perception less impaired than might be expected. It is true that the process of learning complex shape discrimination of a visual kind is impaired with imbeciles but this may be caused by deficient attention and learning. Certainly motor handicap would appear to be a more prominent feature of deficit than perceptual impairment. The aspect of discrimination which appears to be most affected is the recognition of close similarities and differences between objects and this disability may be a function of verbal formulation or judgement rather than actual failure to discriminate perceptually.

Imbeciles take longer to *learn* a discrimination but our experiment shows that when learnt it is recognized with great specificness. If this is the case the imbecile's lack of ability to discriminate must be regarded as a function of lack of conceptual abstraction rather than a perceptual disability. Clearly this general conclusion needs reinforcement before we can be confident that the response processes are more seriously handicapped than the sensory. Our own work suggests this and the literature is consistent with such an interpretation.

Another point which emerges from these experiments is the importance of intersensory transfer in perception and learning and the role of verbal coding in this operation. Defectives can perform certain learning operations better when they are obliged to adopt this procedure.

Finally differential sensory impairment does occur notwithstanding anything which we have said above. Different kinds of sensory impairment may be found with different types of subnormality.

Regarding our experimental results, the following conclusions are therefore indicated:

1. After one trial imbeciles equal normal children of like mental age in matching and recognizing designs.
2. After one or two presentations imbeciles are as good as normals of the same mental age in visual discrimination between familiar and novel shapes. Under the same conditions tactile shape discrimination of non-mongoloid imbeciles equals that of normals of the same chronological age.
3. Mongols are worse than non-mongoloid imbeciles of the same I.Q. in tactile shape discrimination and in copying and reproducing designs.
4. More trials are needed for imbeciles than for normal children matched for mental age, to learn consistent discrimination between stimuli differing along an intensity scale. This is true for auditory intensity, brightness and visual size discrimination learning. Once learned, the amount of generalization to neighbouring stimuli is greater in normals.

5. Discrimination learning is accelerated if one increases the dimensions over which stimuli vary from each other. Fewer trials are needed in learning to distinguish a stimulus differing in size and pattern from others, than when it differs in pattern only.

CHAPTER IV

SOME EXPERIMENTS ON WORDS AND COMMUNICATION

In the previous chapter we raised the question of the role of words in intersensory coding and transfer.

The development of interest in language, partly as a function of the problems it presents for communication engineers, has given a new direction to studies in thinking, memory and concept formation. Miller (1951) for example has attempted to show how words and thoughts are associated and Bartlett (1958), Bruner, Goodnow and Austen (1956) and Osgood, Suci and Tannenbaum (1957) have all given new interpretations of the meaning of meaning. Each of these has made significant advances on Humphrey's (1948) survey of thinking as subvocal speech. Humphrey's view was cautious, showing how language permeated thinking but refusing to identify the two. Osgood and Bruner both stress the dependence of some aspects of meaning on verbal association and Miller says, "Thinking is never more precise than the language it uses". Mowrer (1954) takes the view that meaning is a function of conditioning and Staats and Staats (1957, 1958) have differentiated between a word's meaning and its verbal associations. The meaning of a word, they contend, is associated originally with experience of the environment and not in the first place with the word's verbal associates. This is an important qualification of meaning and symbolism, and must be taken into account in evaluating such a statement as that quoted from Miller. From some points of view it will certainly be the case that not all thinking will be mediated by words or any other group of symbols.

Weakness in the development of speech and language in subnormals has been recognized and described by Tredgold (1952) and others. More recent experimental evidence obtained by Luria (1961) and his colleagues in the Soviet Union suggests however that such patients suffer not only from a lack of development of the verbal or second signalling system, but also from a dissociation between this system and the one governing motor behaviour. This indeed is held by the Soviet psychologists to be the crucial factor in which the mental processes of imbeciles differ from those of normals. Luria states that in such subjects "the system of verbal abstraction does not take its necessary role in the formation of new links and the child's psychic development must inevitably and increasingly take on a deeply pathological character on account of this defect". According to this, two problems in relation to speech would have to be investigated. The first is the meaning of words for imbeciles and the second the connection between words and motor behaviour.

One of the first questions to ask is how many words are actually used by imbeciles in their speech. Mein and O'Connor (1960) have carried out a study comparing the vocabulary of severely subnormal, institutionalized patients with that collected by Burroughs (1957) of normal children. The children in Burroughs' sample were aged between 5 and 6½ years and the imbeciles had mental ages between 3 and 7 years. In both studies a number of interviews were carried out, some of them using picture material as a starting point for conversation. The method of word collection was to note frequency of usage of a particular word. For each individual child a word once used was subsequently ignored because it was not a new word. In these conditions defectives had vocabularies ranging from 106 to 677 different words, average 359, and normals from 56 to 578 with an average of 273. As a result it was possible to produce a list of words used by nearly all children and of words used by only a few. Words which were used by at least half the subjects formed the core—and words by less than half the fringe vocabulary. Mein found that defectives have a larger core vocabulary and a smaller fringe vocabulary than normal children. Thus normals have a greater variety of words at their disposal, while imbeciles have a larger common vocabulary. It seems likely that this difference is a function of the differing mental ages and the restricted environment of the subnormals. Lyle (1960) has shown that imbeciles improve their vocabulary scores when living in a favourable environment.

If we consider the results of Mein's investigation from the point of view of the structure of the language used, its grammatical correctness, one main result emerges. This is that imbeciles, like very young children, use a higher percentage of nouns than of verbs compared with normal children of the same mental age. As mental age increases so does the relative proportion of verbs in the speech of the imbeciles. The following table illustrates this trend.

TABLE 5. GRAMMATICAL STRUCTURE BY GROUPS OF INCREASING MENTAL AGE (NOUNS AND VERBS IN CONVERSATION)

	Mean M.A.			
	3 yr 6 mth	4 yr 8 mth	5 yr 6 mth	6 yr 5 mth
Verbs	18·6	20·0	21·9	20·6
Nouns	31·8	30·8	22·9	21·6

It is a striking conclusion from those results that imbeciles do not differ in the logic of their language development from normal children. This is an interesting fact considering the lack of logic shown in their thinking. But even if the formal structure of the speech of subnormals is similar to that of normal children, words may lack meaning or might have acquired meaning different from that for normals. To test this we have compared the meaning of words for normals and subnormals, using a technique developed by Underwood and Richardson (1956). They presented subjects with a list of nouns and instructed them to give a single association to each word. Only responses in terms of descriptive sense impressions like "round", "hot" or "blue" were allowed. Forty descriptive response categories thus obtained were then listed, and the nouns classified accordingly, each one showing the percentage with which it fell into a certain response category. The word "balloon" for instance elicited the response "round" in 55 per cent of the subjects, "light" in 17 per cent and "rubbery" in 8 per cent. "Brick" resulted in 46 per cent of "red" responses, 35 per cent of "hard", 7 per cent of "square" and 5 per cent of "heavy". Thus, a particular response category, for instance "round", was elicited by such stimuli as "barrel", "doughnut", "cherry", "dome", "pearl" and "cabbage".

Underwood and Richardson make it clear that these percentage frequency values do not necessarily represent the relative strength of responses for a given subject. Only a single response was obtained from the subject for each word. Consequently the knowledge that 50 per cent of the subjects responded with "white" and 20 per cent with "round" to a certain word stimulus does not entail that the 50 per cent who said "white" would, if asked to give a second response, say "round" 20 per cent of the time. But in spite of this and other qualifications this study provides a basis for further work on word scaling.

We were interested in applying this technique to imbeciles to obtain if possible a word scale with approximately equal intervals between response frequencies. In a pilot experiment with normal children we selected three response categories: "round", "white" and "hot", from Underwood and Richardson's list, with seven stimulus words for each concept. Each subject was given only one stimulus word from each of the three scales and in a further attempt to avoid the effects of "set", the order of presentation of the response category to which the respective stimulus words belonged was varied randomly. One hundred and twenty children were tested in the pilot study, so that 40 responses for each word were obtained. A general instruction, asking for descriptive associations was thought to be too complex for the subjects. The stimulus word was therefore presented in such a way as to make a descriptive response likely. Thus the child was asked: "Tell me what milk is like" or "Tell me what a ball is like." Prior to the testing, examples were given to the children in a group. They were asked: "When you came to school this morning, did you see some grass on the way? What was it like?" "Green" was the predominant response. The next example was, "Now tell me what a mountain is like". To this the response was often "White", at which the experimenter said, "Yes, sometimes it is white but not always. What is it always like?" "High" or "big" was accepted as correct and the third example given: "What is the night-time like?" In most instances the response "dark" was obtained. Following this each child was tested individually as described on three words, each of which belonged to one of the three selected concept categories. While scoring the responses it became evident that colour responses predominated to all stimulus words. This was particularly the case with the younger children. The "hot" scale yielded an insufficient number of common responses and consequently words from a "red" scale were substituted in the main experiments.

The aim of the next stage of the investigation was to obtain a five-point scale with equally graded response frequency intervals. Four hundred and forty-eight normal children, aged 5–7 years, and 222 defectives, C.A. 10–20, M.A. 5–7, took part in the scaling experiment. As in the pilot study, a group instruction and examples were given. After this each child was tested individually and was presented with three stimulus words, one from each of the selected response categories. The percentage of each of the category responses for each stimulus word for normals and defectives are given in the following table.

TABLE 6. PERCENTAGE FREQUENCY OF USE OF DESCRIPTIVE
ADJECTIVES IN NORMALS (N = 448) AND SUBNORMALS (N = 222)

Noun stimuli	Adjective responses	% Frequency normals	% Frequency subnormals
Blood	Red	85	85
Tomato		80	71
Fire		53	43
Tongue		23	52
Brick		3	28
Milk	White	83	91
Sheet		83	85
Snow		91	87
Chalk		73	74
Teeth		78	83
Circle	Round	91	71
Hoop		71	65
Ring		57	50
Wheel		53	48
Penny		53	42

As can be seen, frequencies with which individual nouns gave rise to the response "red" were the most regularly spaced of the three scales. If the five words of the red scale are set out along an axis of percentage frequencies the result approximates a straight line. Therefore the red word scale was selected for use in the generalization experiment.

Twenty-four normal and 24 subnormal children acted as subjects. The normals, aged 5–7 years, were pupils at an L.C.C. Infant School. The imbeciles had an age range from 10–20 years, I.Q.s between 33 and 55 and mental ages from 5 to 7 years.

The procedure was as follows: the two stimulus words "blood" and "brick", from the previously established red category scale gave the largest and smallest number of "red" responses. They were repeatedly recorded on a sound tape in random order. The sound level of intensity with which the words were reproduced was constant at 70 dB, with an eight-second time interval between words. The subject had a button in front of him, pressure of which was relayed to a recording milliammeter. A pen recorded each pressure response and a second event pen registered each stimulus word as it was spoken. Half of the number of subjects were required to give a positive response (pressure on the button) to the "high intensity" stimulus word of the scale ("blood") and inhibit such a response to the "low intensity" stimulus word ("brick"). For the remaining half of the subjects this procedure was reversed, "brick" being the positive and "blood" the negative stimulus. When no response to a positive stimulus occurred the experimenter said "Press". If a response was given he said "Good". He also said "Good" if the button was not pressed on the presentation of a negative stimulus. If such an incorrect response did occur he said "No, don't press". Trials were continued up to a criterion of 24 correct responses, 12 of which were positive and 12 negative.

After this criterion was reached, the child was given the following instruction: "Now you are going to hear some more words: those you have heard before as well as some others. If it is a word for a very red thing, like blood, press the button. If it is not so very red, like brick, don't press." This instruction was, of course, reversed for those who had previously been taught to respond positively to "brick". The five words of the "red" scale: "Blood,

Tomato, Fire, Tongue and Brick", were then presented. Each child heard each stimulus word ten times, and the 50 words were presented in random order by the tape recorder.

Frequency of a motor response to any one word was used as a measure of generalization. For the purpose of comparing the slope of the obtained generalization curve with that of the scale, "negative responses", i.e. absence of pressure, after a word when previously conditioned to respond positively to "brick" were scored in such a manner as to make them equivalent to positive ones when originally conditioned to "blood". Frequencies and percentages of responses to each stimulus word for normals and defectives are given in the following table.

TABLE 7. PERCENTAGE GENERALIZATION FOLLOWING CONDITIONING OF "BLOOD" FOR NORMALS (N = 24) AND SUBNORMALS (N = 24)

	Normals	Subnormals
Blood	100	94
Tomato	90	70
Fire	46	53
Tongue	45	43
Brick	3	8

Two aspects of the results from this investigation should be considered. One is that scaling of words in the manner described is validated by the close similarity of the slopes of the category scale and the generalization curves. A comparison of the two previous tables shows that the frequency with which each of the five words results in the association "red", and the frequency with which generalization of a conditioned motor response to these words occurs is closely paralleled.

This points to the possibility of developing verbal scales of varying character and complexity—for instance, evaluative as well as descriptive ones—which might be used in concept formation experiments, in studies which aim to compare verbal with non-verbal behaviour and possibly also in clinical assessments. That such comparatively crude methods as have been described result in a verbal scale which is validated in a subsequent experiment is

encouraging. This means that the amount of semantic generalization of the concept "red" generalizes along a magnitude scale in
a manner similar to other non-verbal stimuli. The more frequently
the response "red" is given to a particular noun by one sample of
children, the more frequently a response conditioned to one word
is generalized to these same nouns by another group.

From these results it may be concluded that verbal generalization in imbecile children follows much the same course as it
does in normals of comparable mental age. Luria's theory that
"meaningful verbal systems" can rarely be built up in such children
might be too pessimistic a view. Although it should be remembered
that we were dealing with high-grade imbeciles only, the assumption can be made that most of these children had cortical anomalies
of varying extent and nature. It seems that such lesions in con-
junction with severe mental subnormality, do not necessarily
prevent the perception of semantic relationships. The relative
similarity of the performance of normal 5–7-year-olds and imbecile
10–20-year-olds emphasizes the fact that words are used correctly by imbeciles within the limits of their vocabularies.

This impression is further reinforced by another experiment
which was carried out to test a similar hypothesis. This was
based on the principle of interference in learning and recall. It
has been a common finding that semantic generalization replaces
phonic generalization with increasing maturity. Results of this
kind have been noted by Razran (1939), Riess (1946) and others.
Luria (1961), as noted earlier, differentiated normals and imbeciles
on such a criterion. Cofer and Foley (1942) varied the character of
interpolated word lists to test the effect on recall of previously
learned words. Although the results were not clearcut the largest
number of words affected were those following interpolated
homonym lists. The second largest were those following synonyms
and the least easily affected were those following an interpolated
control list.

O'Connor and Hermelin (1959,a) used a group of 30 imbecile
children with average I.Q. 40 and with an I.Q. range from 30 to
50 points. Their ages ranged from 9 to 16 years with a mean of
12 years. They were without gross motor or sensory handicap.
The material consisted of a list of six christian names used for
matching purposes, three different training lists, and one common

test list. While no obvious relationship existed between the neutral list (N) and the test list (T), list (M) contained words of similar meaning to those in the common test list, and (S) was related by sound similarity to the test list. The words used were:

(Matching)	(N)	(M)	(S)	(T)
Peter	Child	Food	Heel	Meal
John	School	Frock	Mess	Dress
Mary	Window	Trousers	Ants	Pants
Kenneth	Star	City	Brown	Town
Ann	Cat	Lorry	Duck	Truck
Michael	Ball	Street	Boat	Road

The subjects had to learn to repeat each set, containing six words, by the method of serial anticipation. The experimenter spoke the first three words of a given set with one-second intervals between words. The subject was then asked to repeat them. If he failed to recall the three words correctly, in the correct order, they were again spoken by the experimenter. When one correct repetition occurred, the full list of six words was presented. After each repetition trial by the subject, the list was re-presented by the experimenter until four consecutive faultless repetitions were given. Each correct repetition was rewarded by a sweet and by the experimenter saying "Good". On each incorrect attempt the experimenter said: "No. I will tell you the words again."

The subjects were first tested on the list of christian names. They were ranked according to the number of trials needed to learn to criterion. Matched triplets were formed, one of each of whom was allotted at random to one of three groups. Another trial session followed in which one of the three training lists and the common test material had to be learned. The training list for each group differed in its relationship to the test list (T), which was the same for all subjects. The control group learned two word lists which were not connected (N+T). The second group was presented with two lists of meaningful similarity so that the relationship between them was semantic (M+T), while the remaining subjects learned two similar sounding lists of words (S+T). The two word lists followed each other after a time interval of five minutes, during which subject and experimenter talked about matters unrelated to the experiment.

The results can be seen from the table of difference scores calculated by subtracting the number of trials required to learn corresponding words in the training and test lists.

TABLE 8. DIFFERENCES IN NUMBER OF TRIALS BETWEEN TWO WORD LISTS

Control group	Semantic group	Sound group
N—T	M—T	S—T
0	−2	+2
0	0	+4
0	−6	+2
−2	−4	+5
0	−8	0
0	−2	+1
0	−7	+7
0	−4	+7
0	−4	0
−1	−2	−1
$\overline{X}$ −0·3	−3·9	+2·7

The groups differed not only in amount and direction of change, but also in the qualitative nature of the effects of training on test words. Failure of word repetition in the case of the N+T and S+T groups was characterized by omission of words. Interference leading to incorrect responses was evident in the M+T group. In this group, subjects frequently substituted words which were first learned for the appropriate meaningfully similar ones in the subsequent task. Thus, while first having had to learn "street" and subsequently "road", the child often said "street" in both instances. Such negative transfer occurred at a mean of 2·0 instances during the learning of the test list, while none was evident with any of the other groups.

The effect of word learning on subsequent meaningfully similar

words suggests two conclusions. Some generalization along semantic dimensions seems to take place in this experiment, and secondly
such generalization becomes effective in the form of interference.
In addition the effect of learning semantically connected words
was apparent after a time interval. In an association experiment,
those who had previously learned the semantically related words
gave mainly meaningfully related word associations. Sound or
"clang" associations were less frequent than previous research
would lead us to expect. Training in semantically connected word
learning seemed to result in a "set". A set resulting from a well
established connection is very stable and long lived. Such a finding
of the persistence of meaningful connections could be of importance in any practical training programme.

These experiments seem to us to give a strong indication of the
capacity which imbeciles have to meaningfully associate and
connect words which they know. The vocabulary scores of imbeciles in hospital show that they are limited in the number of
words which they can use and as a result the number of connections which they can make. This fact seems to be basic to any
practical teaching techniques. Such practical applications will be
discussed in a later chapter but it is appropriate to refer to another
study at this point which shows the directions of such a practical
application.

Reading ability of children in a mental deficiency hospital was
tested in this study (Hermelin and O'Connor 1960,a). The hypothesis was that words used frequently in speech would be more
readily decoded from printed symbols, i.e. would be easier to read
than words which were not used in speech. Thirty-two patients
of imbecile grade were used in the study. Their average age was
15 years. The procedure consisted simply of asking the subjects
to read printed words. The words were of a known frequency of
occurrence in imbecile speech and were chosen to represent all
ranges of frequency from Mein's word list. The fact which is
of interest to us is that words which occur in the speech of
74–100 per cent of imbeciles were read by 68 per cent of the
subjects in this survey, but those used by 50–73 per cent were
read by only 24 per cent. A highly significant relationship between
spoken vocabulary and reading skill is shown ($P < 0.001$). However
it should be noted that the length of a word is also closely related

E

to the frequency with which it is used. The shorter the word, the greater the frequency (Zipf, 1935).

A poor vocabulary and the disinclination to use words as mental tools indicates that enlarging the imbeciles' vocabulary as well as strengthening the connection between verbal and perceptual motor behaviour is crucial in any educational programme. We have demonstrated that if these factors are taken into account, imbeciles can be taught to read a limited number of words and sentences with understanding. To illustrate this the table below shows reading scores of eight imbecile children, aged between 11 and 15 with I.Q.s from 35 to 49. The children have, for the last year, attended daily reading lessons, each lesson lasting for 20 minutes. They were taught to read words and sentences from the spoken vocabulary list of Mein.

TABLE 9. READING TEST SCORES OVER ONE YEAR BASED ON 200 WORD LIST

S	1st Test Oct-Nov 1960	2nd Test Feb 1961	3rd Test July 1961	4th Test Nov 1961
1	6	24	48	80
2	14	22	47	63
3	4	14	28	42
4	5	10	28	51
5	7	36	71	103
6	35	63	87	110
7	5	22	57	91
8	35	51	70	94

The subjects were tested at the beginning of this period, and at four subsequent intervals. The increases in reading scores are highly significant at each stage. Bad starters seem to improve at about the same rate as good starters, and there is no indication yet that any of the children have reached the limit of their achievement. Reading can be improved if based on a meaningful spoken vocabulary as this table shows.

One conclusion to be drawn from this chapter is that whereas semantic associations can be formed by imbeciles, the verbal material on which they draw is limited. If however this short-coming could be surmounted, associational complexity might follow. This possibility would make it worth while for us to overcome the initial input difficulty.

Alternatively, the main difficulty may be not so much in lack of connections within the verbal system, as in a lack of connection between that system and the one controlling motor behaviour. Imbeciles are rarely able to verbalize strategies and principles of solution in problem solving tasks. Nor can they make effective use of a general verbal instruction. In some of the subsequent experiments this connection between verbal and motor behaviour will be investigated.

Our conclusions from these studies are:

1. The restricted vocabulary of institutionalized imbeciles is at least partly due to their limited and limiting environment. The structure of the language used by them resembles that of normal children at a corresponding stage of mental development.
2. If imbeciles use a word in speech, it has the same semantic characteristics as it has for normals of like mental age. Word associations to nouns fall into the same descriptive response categories for normals and subnormals.
3. Semantic generalization does occur in imbeciles. The effect of learning meaningfully related words is evident in subsequent word associations. Learning sets can be established, which favour the meaningful verbal connections rather than random or "clang" associations.
4. Words which are used by imbeciles in their speech are easier read than words not so used. Knowledge of the meaning of a word facilitates recognition of it in printed form.

CHAPTER V

THOUGHT AND LANGUAGE

FOR our present purposes we will confine the term "thinking" to that process which takes place when a subject seeks to solve a problem. In studying the thought processes of severely subnormal children we have thus been less concerned with level of attainment, or with what such children could do, than with how they did it, i.e. with the nature of their problem-solving strategies.

Bartlett (1958) suggests that it may be useful for the experimental psychologist to begin his investigations of thinking by regarding it as a high level skill. The role of properties and variables, which have been found to be relevant to the attainment and performance of skills could then be investigated in their relation to thinking.

Clarke (1958) summarizing the abilities and trainability of imbeciles in regard to motor skills, mentions the following factors amongst others. He says that:

(1) Subjects must be well motivated, and the most effective motivation seems to be the setting of a realistic goal. This, in relation to problem-solving tasks would mean that problems should not be so easy as to be boring and not be so difficult as to lead to excessive fatigue and frustration. Knowledge of results should be provided.

(2) The task to be learned needs to be broken down to its basic constituents. This would imply a distinct series of steps, the successful accomplishment of each being dependent on mastering the previous one. The importance of the right sequence must be stressed.

(3) Spaced learning and need for over-learning. These principles, which have been found useful for the acquisition of skills, have also proved valid for learning conceptual and abstract material.

56

(4) The importance of verbal reinforcement.

This last point in our view is central to the impairments which severely subnormals show in their thinking. The role of language may be decisive for the degree of efficiency with which imbeciles may be able to master problems as distinct from acquiring skills. Whereas motor skill can be acquired by a process akin to conditioning, problem solving behaviour may depend on recognizing a principle of solution and its verbal formulation. If we consider how severely subnormal children think, one of the basic questions is whether and how they make use of concepts and categories. Bruner (1957) suggests that the learning and utilization of categories represents one of the most elementary and general forms of cognition by which man adjusts to his environment. Categorizing he says is essentially a form of coding, a means by which objects and events in the environment are identified according to features which they either share or do not share with other events or objects. Bruner agrees with Seguin that the process by which perceptual attributes are utilized for classification is not qualitatively different from the one using conceptual or abstract attributes. He points to the distinction between concept formation and concept attainment. According to him, concept formation is the attempt to sort items into some set of meaningful classes, any meaningful set of classes which orders their diversity. Concept attainment on the other hand refers to the process of finding predictive defining attributes distinguishing exemplars from nonexemplars of the class one seeks to discriminate.

Thus the organism, while coding the stimuli in his environment continuously goes "beyond the information given", utilizing past and predicting future events. Transfer of a principle of solution from one problem to another may also be defined as a coding operation. Nothing according to this is really being transferred. The organism is learning codes that have narrower or wider applicability. Much of what Bruner calls coding we call classifying, using the term coding in a narrower sense. Coding such as we describe in the next chapter would generally involve only translation and not necessarily classification although occasionally both are involved.

How far are severely subnormal children able to use classifying principles as a mental tool and to what extent are they able to apply an acquired concept to solve a subsequent problem? House and Zeaman (1958) suggest that there is no evidence that learning sets are built up in discrimination tasks, and that imbeciles are rather worse than apes in their transfer ability. However, Tizard and Loos (1954), Barnett and Cantor (1957), Clarke and Blakemore (1961) and Clarke and Cookson (1962) obtained more positive results. Clarke *et al.* found that young imbecile children showed massive transfer effects in sorting abstract, non-representational designs. They conclude that what was transferred could be defined as learning set, as well as sharpened perceptual and conceptual discrimination. Hermelin and O'Connor (1958) have carried out an experiment which investigated whether severely subnormal children would find it easier to discriminate between stimuli by applying a principle of classification than by a process of rote memory. We also asked if the principle of using a classifying category could be transferred from one task to another.

Procedure was based on an experiment by Gentry, Kaplan and Iscoe (1956) who compared monkeys and children on different learning tasks. While one task could be solved by rote memory only, the other could be dealt with by that method, or by the recognition of a common element in certain presented designs. It was found that all human subjects, in contrast to the monkeys in Gentry's study, were able to employ the "principle of solution" and thus effectively improve the rate of learning.

In our experiment 20 clinically heterogeneous institutionalized male imbecile children acted as subjects. They were divided into two groups of 10, with mean C.A. 12·9 years, range 10·3–16·4, and mean I.Q. 40·7, range 28–50. Of these 20, 9 had no recognized clinical anomalies. Of the remaining 11, 5 showed physiological or biochemical abnormalities, 2 were mongols and 4 were diagnosed epileptics with brain damage.

The material consisted of six series of pictures, each series containing 12 different simple black outline drawings. They were presented in pairs, on a sliding tray, each pair containing one "correct" and one "incorrect" picture. A sweet was hidden in a small well under the correct picture so that its choice was rewarded. Instructions to the children were to try to find the picture under which the sweet was hidden. Each child was tested individually, and each of the six series containing six pairs of pictures each, was presented for 20 trials. Before the tests started, each child was asked to name each pictured object in order to assure his familiarity with the represented items. All subjects could do this without difficulty.

The material fell into three categories, each represented by two series (Ia, Ib, IIa, IIb, IIIa, IIIb). In Ia and Ib the correct pictures were arbitrarily chosen and could consequently only be learned and remembered by a process of rote memory. In IIa and IIb the concept to be generalized was that of an object belonging to a certain class, the rewarded picture of a pair always showing "a piece of furniture" in IIa, and "an animal" in IIb. In the last category a more abstract concept of quantity had to be evolved, and "three objects of a kind" in series IIIa and "more than one object" in IIIb were pictured on the reward card. The position of the rewarded card in a pair was varied randomly from trial to trial. While one group of 10 subjects was presented with the material in order:

1. Rote material (Ia, Ib),
2. "Concrete concept" (IIa = "furniture", IIb = "animals"),
3. "Abstract concept" (IIIa = "three of a kind", IIIb = "more than one"),

The other group was given:

1. Abstract concepts (IIIa, IIIb),
2. Concrete concepts (IIa, IIb),
3. Rote material (Ia, Ib).

Thus, while the order of presenting two instances of related concepts "a" and "b" *within* each kind of material was maintained, order of presentation *between* different kinds of material was reversed for the second group. It seemed reasonable to expect that this simple experimental design would give us an indication of whether or not imbeciles could learn to use principles of classification under the stated stimulus conditions.

The results indicate that the subjects employed simple principles of classification effectively enough to facilitate rates of discrimination learning. Mean scores for the number of trials at which the subjects reached and maintained the maximum score of 6 are given in the following table. If a series had not been learned after 20 trials a score of 21 was assumed.

Significant differences in the rate of learning exist between concept and rote series in both groups. The learning curves of the mean number of correct responses on any trial for the different types of material show different characteristics—curves for rote material rise gradually, and straight lines can be fitted to them. For concept material on the other hand all curves but one show a sharp initial rise, the exception being one with an unusually high starting point in this particular series. Thus it seems justified to conclude that the quality of the learning process has been different in the two instances.

TABLE 10. NUMBER OF TRIALS NEEDED TO REACH AND MAINTAIN MAXIMUM CORRECT SCORES

Material	Rote		Concrete concepts		Abstract concepts	
	(Ia)	(Ib)	(IIa)	(IIb)	(IIIa)	(IIIb)
Group 1						
Order of						
presentation	1	2	3	4	5	6
Mean	18·8	17·1	12·5	11·1	9·5	6·3
S.D.	2·64	4·23	4·80	5·99	5·79	4·63
Group 2						
Order of						
presentation	5	6	3	4	1	2
Mean	17·8	16·9	10·3	11·0	12·9	5·4
S.D.	2·14	2·12	4·91	5·74	5·56	5·83

The position of any one task in the series does not significantly alter the speed with which it is learned, while, as can be seen from the table, irrespective of its position, concept material is always learned in fewer trials than rote. Therefore, it seemed justified to treat the two groups as one in investigating possible transfer effects. If we compare the tasks within each group, i.e. Ia with Ib, IIa with IIb and IIIa with IIIb, there is no significant difference between the two rote series (Ia and Ib), nor between the two series representing "concrete" concepts (IIa and IIb).

There is, however, a difference between the two abstract concept series (IIIa and IIIb). The scores in the second abstract concept series (IIIb) are the lowest for any material, which seems to indicate that the subjects had the least difficulty with a task which, in Heidbreder's (1928) experiments, represents the most abstract and difficult kind of concept. The reason may be that the two quantitative series were more alike than the "concrete" examples.

Of the 20 children, 15 spontaneously named the illustrated objects in any one series as soon as they had memorized the correct discrimination response. Once naming in this manner had commenced, correct responses were maintained by 13 out of the 15 subjects. Only 2 of the 20 children could, however, account verbally for the principle according to which they made their choices. The other 18 were quite unable, even on insistent questioning, to formulate the principle, according to which correct responses had occurred.

This experiment seems to indicate that imbecile children are able to use simple concepts as principles of solution, yet their ability to classify and take note of essential similarities is relatively divorced from their ability to formulate such principles verbally.

Hull (1920) reports that "mentally abnormals" show an almost complete inability to define a concept and that even with normals the ability to define is not necessarily a true index of a concept's functional value. Verplanck (personal communication) obtained a similar indication from card-sorting experiments with normal adults and children. On the other hand, investigations reported by Luria (1961) and experiments such as the one by Spiker, Gerynoy and Shepard (1956) seem to suggest that verbal definition assists the attainment of a concept. The extent and limit of the "conceptualizing ability" of imbeciles, as well as the role which language could play to assist and further it, will have to be determined.

The role of verbalization in problem solving was investigated in another experiment which compared normal and subnormal children on a reversal task.

In reversal experiments a stimulus choice is usually rewarded until it is consistently made, whereupon the reward is shifted to the previously negative stimulus. Transfer in such a situation should be negative, and the subject begins to learn the reversal task with a considerable handicap. It might be said that in the same manner as a positive stimulus acquires excitatory response tendencies during training, a negative one gives rise to inhibition. This inhibition would first have to be dispersed before new excitatory tendencies towards the formerly negative stimulus could become effective.

In experiments with the feebleminded, consistent differences between them and normals of comparable mental age have not usually been found in the rate of discrimination and reversal learning. Gardner (1945), who trained her subjects to choose one out of three differently marked boxes, found a decrement in the number of correct responses for all I.Q. levels when the reward was shifted to a previously incorrect box. Idiots seemed to have had greater difficulties in this task than the other subnormal subjects. Plenderleith (1956) required her subjects to learn to choose one of two stimuli in a consistent fashion; after this discrimination was learned, the subjects were required to shift their responses to the previously incorrect stimulus. The feebleminded children did not differ significantly from the normals in either discrimination trials or in the reversal scores for trials given after 24 hours. Stevenson and Ziegler's (1957) subjects were trained to select one out of three stimuli; following different degrees of training, they were switched to a new size discrimination involving the same stimuli. Normal children, feebleminded children, and feebleminded adults did not differ significantly in the acquisition of the first solution, nor in their performance on the second problem. No significant differences appeared as a function of degree of training. Kounin (1948) reported that feebleminded subjects reversed a motor response faster than normals. His subjects were, however, *instructed* to reverse the response, and it is questionable if his experimental conditions made a comparison with other reversal experiments meaningful. He interpreted his results in terms of such concepts as "functional rigidity" and "a high barrier between psychological regions", which prevent interference from previously acquired response patterns. The same concept of rigidity could, of course, be applied to explain exactly opposite behaviour manifestations. Less mobile systems might result in difficulty for the subject to reverse an established discrimination response.

In our experiment (O'Connor and Hermelin 1959,b), black squares of different sizes were used as stimuli. They were presented, two at a time, on a tray on which they could be moved to reveal a reward. The squares were painted on red cardboard, each card measuring 20×20 cm. The size of the squares differed by a ratio of $5:8$. A sweet was given as reward for every correct response. After the trials had been completed, each child was asked to give a verbal account of the principle according to which he made his choices.

In the discrimination trials, half the subjects in each group were rewarded for choosing the smaller stimulus; the others were rewarded for choosing the larger of the two squares. Trials continued until 10 consecutive correct responses occurred. Immediately after the criterion for discrimination was reached, and without any comment by the experimenter, the subjects were given a number of reversal trials in which the formerly negative of the two stimuli was the correct rewarded choice. The reversal trials continued until 10 correct consecutive choices were made.

Ten institutionalized imbecile children and 10 normal children acted as subjects. The imbeciles had a mean I.Q. of 42 (range, 33–50), a mean CA of 11·5 years (range, 9–15), and a mean MA of 4·9 years (range, 3·4–6·7). The control group consisted of normal school children with a mean CA of 5·1.

TABLE 11. MEAN ACQUISITION AND REVERSAL SCORES FOR NORMALS AND IMBECILES

	Discrimination	Reversal
First experiment:		
Normals	31·5 ± 24·9	25·4 ± 16·6
Imbeciles	39·6 ± 24·7	11·0 ± 5·2
Second experiment:		
Imbeciles	25·1 ± 13·7	39·6 ± 27·0

Differences between the discrimination scores of the two groups were not significant. The crucial difference between the two groups in this experiment is evident in the reversal trials. While the imbeciles needed only a mean of 11 trials to reverse successfully a previously learned response, the normals required a mean of 25·4 trials. This difference is even more pronounced if one relates it to the original discrimination scores of the two groups. While the normals need nearly as many trials again for reversal as for discrimination, the imbeciles need less than a third of the number of trials for reversal compared with discrimination. The difference between normal and imbecile reversal scores is significant at the 0·01 level, and while no significant difference is apparent between discrimination and reversal scores in the normal group, this difference reaches a significance level of 0·05 for the imbeciles.

Eight of the 10 normal children could formulate the relevant verbal hypothesis of size discrimination either spontaneously or when asked, whereas in no instance was the experimenter able to elicit the principle from any of the imbecile children, excepting one child who stated it spontaneously.

As a tentative explanation of this finding, it was hypothesized that the normal child tends to formulate the solution to the problem verbally: for example, "the sweet is always under the big square". In the reversal task, this verbal self-instruction comes into conflict with the new reinforcement and interferes with the solution of the task. What seems to be required of the child is some unlearning of a previously established response tendency before new learning can take place.

The imbecile child, on the other hand, supposedly never formulated a verbal hypothesis; therefore, he might be able to respond more immediately to the reinforcement coming from the direct stimuli. Response tendencies formed without the participation of the verbal system might be less stable and extinguish faster than those formed with the additional verbal formula. If the inability of imbeciles to use words as guiding hypotheses was a determining factor in the results, training and reinforcing such verbalization should slow down the reversal process and bring the scores nearer to those obtained by the normal children.

The discrimination-reversal experiment was repeated with another group of 10 imbeciles, matched in age and I.Q. with the previous one. Whereas no comments were made with the previous groups during the trials each correct discrimination response was verbally reinforced with the second group. Whenever the child responded correctly, he was asked, "Under which picture did you find the sweet? Under the big or under the little one?" If the response was "This", with pointing, the next question was, "Which one is this?" On the response "The big one" or "The little one", it was again asked, "Tell me again now, under which picture was the sweet?" Questioning persisted until the child gave the correct verbal account, and the same procedure was repeated after every correct motor response.

No questions were asked or comments made during the reversal trials, which, as previously, followed immediately after the criterion in the discrimination task was reached.

In the acquisition task, this second group needed a mean of 25·1 to reach the required discrimination criterion, compared with 39·6 trials for the imbeciles and 31·5 for the normals in the previous experiment. These differences are, however, statistically non-significant.

Previously, normal reversal and discrimination scores had been statistically equal, and the imbeciles needed significantly *fewer* trials for reversal than for discrimination. As was the case with the normal children, the difference between discrimination and reversal scores was not significant for the second group of imbeciles. Their reversal scores differ significantly from those of the first group ($P = 0·01$) and are not significantly different from those of the normals.

At the beginning little connection between verbal and motor behaviour was evident with the second group of subnormal children. Thus, for instance, after responding correctly, a child would state, equally correctly, that he had found the sweet under the larger square. He would then choose the smaller one at the next trial, and finding no reward, would say, "It is under the big one". Yet the next response would again be incorrect, although the child was quite able to point to the larger stimulus square when asked to do so. However, the connections between the two kinds of response were gradually formed, and the children tended to advance a hypothesis as to where the reward would be before making the motor response. They would spontaneously say, "It is under the big one", and would then make the correct choice.

When the stimulus situation was reversed, the previously appropriate verbal response tended to persist as a stereotype, although it was no longer an adequate guide to motor behaviour. Nevertheless, the subjects, although still using previously learned and now inappropriate verbal regulations, gradually reversed their choice behaviour, responding to the direct signals. But while reversing to the newly correct smaller stimulus, they still would say, "It is under the big one". However, gradually some of the children were able to reverse their verbal response—two simultaneously with and one immediately following the motor reversals. Four gradually stopped any verbal comment, and three persisted in the verbal stereotype previously acquired until the end of the trials. For those subjects, the verbal system seemed to have lost its regulating, orienting role in relation to the direct signals.

Pavlov described two signal systems in the human organism, one governed by non-verbal and the other by verbal stimuli. In the normal child, the second system develops to dominate and guide response to almost all direct signals. If one assumes with Luria and his colleagues that in certain forms of disease either lack of development in one of the systems or lack of fusion between the two is a prominent symptom, then decreased mobility as well as instability of certain responses become explicable. Applied to the present investigation this formulation suggests that while conditioning with the influence of the verbal system takes place more quickly than without it, the connections thus developed are less mobile than those established on the basis of direct signals alone.

The experiment seems to show that the imbeciles, as long as they are not verbally reinforced, learn a perceptual motor habit, whereas the normals acquire two habits, one perceptual motor and one verbal. It must be borne in mind that the mean age of the normal group in this experiment was just 5 years, the stage of development at which, according to Luria, verbal self-regulation of behaviour is just beginning. Older children would presumably be able to adapt their verbal as well as their motor behaviour to a changed stimulus situation with more facility. However, with this particular age group of normals, as well as with imbecile children, words seemed to be a powerful determinant preventing them from reversing "set" rapidly. Conversely, lack of verbal regulation of motor activity in imbeciles seemed to result in unstable responses which could be rapidly reversed. A verbal habit, once set up in accordance with the motor one, lacks mobility and slows down reversal.

The effect of "set" was demonstrated in an experiment by Hermelin (1958) which aimed to transfer a verbal response given to a pictured object to the written word nominating it.

Ten subnormal children, aged 10·3 to 15 years, mean 12·6 with I.Q.s 35–50, mean 43·6, acted as subjects. Four three-letter words were chosen. They were written in large capital letters on white cardboard cards 6 in. by 4 in. An additional card showed a simple pictorial illustration of the word, and a further one displayed this picture as well as the written word naming it. There were also two words for each of the four to be learned, which varied from them by one letter only. The words are given below:

Words to be associated with a picture			
BED	COW	DOG	CUP

Words used for discrimination			
RED	BOW	HOG	CAP
BAD	COT	DOT	CUT

The aim, in this part of the experiment, was to transfer the response of naming the picture to the naming of the written word. The subject was told that he was going to be shown some cards through a window in a screen, and was asked to tell the experimenter what was on the card every time it was presented. All correct responses were rewarded with a sweet. In addition the experimenter said "good" for a correct response. The procedure was to present first the picture, then the picture with the name of the object written on the same card, and finally the written word alone. Trials were continued until five consecutive naming responses to each of the three cards (picture, word and picture, word) had occurred. Then the card which showed word and picture together was eliminated, and a further five correct responses to each of the remaining two cards, the picture, and the written word naming it, were required. The same procedure was followed with the other three words. The order in which words were presented was randomly varied from subject to subject.

After the criterion of 10 consecutive correct responses was reached, the subject was immediately presented with the discrimination task, which formed the second stage of the experiment. Each of the words to which a response had previously been established was in turn presented with two scripturally similar ones. The card with the "correct" word written on it was also given, and the subject was asked: show me which of those three words says "bed" ("dog", "cow", "cup"). Each incorrect choice was corrected. If, after three trials responses were still incorrect, the subject was asked to trace the letters of the "correct" word with his finger. Trials were repeated, the position of the cards displaying the three words varying randomly, until the subject made 10 correct choices in succession. The process was then repeated with the remaining previously presented three words.

The third stage consisted of a word recognition test in which the subject was presented three times with the list of the previously learned four words. He was asked to say what was on each card. The number of correct responses out of a possible total of 12 was recorded.

Four of the 10 children were able to recognize some letters in the reading test, but none could read any of the words at the 4-year-old level. Except for one subject, the ability to recognize single letters was not correlated with word recognition in the experiment.

All 10 subjects gave the required verbal response at the first presentation of the pictured object, as well as to the second stimulus presented, the pictured object with the additional lettering. The mean number of presentations needed to transfer this response to the card showing only the letters was 4·7 for the first word (range 1–12), 1·9 for the second and 1·3 and 1·1 for the third and fourth respectively. It seems that a "learning set" became quickly effective and enabled the subjects to respond almost immediately in an appropriate manner to the subsequent presentations of written words.

Subjects needed a mean number of 10·7 trials (range 1–30) before the first word was correctly discriminated from the two other, similar ones. For the three following words, however, error scores were only 1·4, 1·8 and 2·8 respectively. Transfer from the first discrimination task to the following ones was thus very marked.

Finally, the subjects were presented three times in succession with the cards containing the four written words. The position of the cards was changed randomly. The subject was asked to read the words on the cards and correct responses were rewarded. The mean number of errors out of a possible 12 was 2·6, five subjects obtaining a score of 10 correct responses. Errors ranged from 0 to 6.

The results of the experiment seem to show that imbecile children can be taught to use and recognize symbolic material in the form of written words. Formerly meaningless patterns of lines, or at best meaningless combination of letters, evoked, by the end of the experiment, the same verbal response as a pictorial representation. The subjects succeeded in transferring the newly established bond between symbols and words to new material. They also learned to discriminate between scripturally similar words and transferred this process of discrimination readily.

It is of interest, that while the first conditioning stage in the experiment was correlated significantly with C.A., the second discrimination stage showed a relationship with intelligence level. It seems that in a task which required for its solution the forming of a new association between a picture and the written symbols designating it, age is a relevant factor. On the other hand, intelligence seems to be a relevant factor in enabling a subject to make a precise discrimination between material which is not pictorial but symbolically representative. What is perhaps even more important than the character and interpretation of those relationships is, that they both refer only to the first encounter with the task, and become non-significant in subsequent presentation of material. It thus seems that findings which suggest that transferability is relatively independent of I.Q. in normals as well as defectives are substantiated in this experiment.

This result and the previous ones demonstrate the importance of the linking of problem-solving behaviour and the verbal reflection of it. Without such verbal parallelism, flexibility exists but responses are more easily extinguished. The experimental series also demonstrate the existence of transfer in imbeciles, even without verbal formulation of the principle of solution.

We can now summarize the findings from these experiments. These are:

F

1. Severely subnormal children can use concepts as principle of classification, though they may be unable to verbalize such concepts.
2. Absence of verbalization leaves a learned perceptual motor response unstable and easily reversible. Reinforcing verbalization leads to a stable and persistent "set" which is difficult to reverse.
3. Naming can be transferred from a picture to the written word designating it. Symbols can be taught to evoke the same verbal response as the things they symbolize.
4. Discrimination between the learned written word and other similar ones can be taught. A "discrimination set" is transferred to other instances.

CHAPTER VI

CROSS MODAL "CODING"

As Luria (1961) has suggested, the bond between the verbal system and motor behaviour is insufficiently developed in imbeciles. The translation of stimuli from one modality to another without changing their meaning, and the reflection of objects and events in the second signalling system have been called by us coding processes. The following experiments attempt to make such coding operations inherent aspects of the tasks to be carried out.

Although imbeciles are impaired in many activities, the verbal system and those activities which involve coding, classification and the use of symbols seem particularly affected. Motor activity can often be substantially improved with suitable training methods. Therefore, it was thought possible that the combined verbal-motor responses of imbeciles might show improvement if compared with verbal behaviour alone. The assumption underlying this hypothesis was that a relatively intact motor system might act as support and reinforcement for verbal behaviour.

Tikhomirova (1956) and Nepomnyashchaya (1956) studied the role of speech and motor behaviour in the severely subnormal. They show that imbecile children tend to respond to a direct rather than to a verbal signal if these are in conflict.

Hermelin and O'Connor (1960,b) carried out an experiment in which the experimental and control groups were each divided into four subgroups. In subgroups 1 and 2, the stimulus was one or two pencil taps, in subgroups 3 and 4 the stimulus was counting aloud "one" or "one, two". Throughout the experiment the subject had to respond by making two responses if one signal was given and one response if two signals were given.

In trials 1–10 and 31–40 responses were tapping or counting alone and in trials 11–30 they were combined tapping and counting.

The responses made by each group in each stage of the experiment are shown in the table.

TABLE 12

Groups	Stimulus	Responses		
		Trials 1–10	Trials 11–30	Trials 31–40
1	Tapping	Tap	Tap and Count	Tap
2		Count	Tap and Count	Count
3	Counting	Count	Count and Tap	Count
4		Tap	Count and Tap	Tap

Forty imbeciles and 20 normals matched for mental age participated in this experiment. The results did not in fact show the primacy of direct signals with imbeciles. Rather they showed the relative effectiveness of responses given in the "opposite" modality from the stimulus. Thus the "tapping-signal, verbal-response" arrangement and the "verbal-signal, tapping-response" arrangement gave better results than the tap-tap or count-count arrangements.

The table illustrates this finding for the imbeciles. The effect is not shown by controls.

TABLE 13. MEAN NUMBER OF CORRECT RESPONSES (MAXIMUM 5)

Stimulus		Responses	
		Tapping	Counting
Tapping	Imbeciles	2·1	3·0
	Controls	4·6	4·0
Counting	Imbeciles	3·4	1·6
	Controls	3·9	4·5

An examination of this simplified table of results which excludes the combined scores for tapping plus counting (trials 11–30) shows that for the tapping stimulus the correct tapping response of the imbeciles is low, but that for the counting response it is higher. For the counting stimulus the score of the imbecile tapping response is high and the counting response lower. Normal controls, however, scarcely vary from condition to condition. Results seem to suggest that as far as imbeciles are concerned there is an inherent compulsion to imitate any stimulus of this kind. However, this is partly overcome if a response must be given in some form other than that in which the stimulus was administered.

We had asked whether the motor system could be activated to reinforce speech reactions. In this way the weakness in the imbeciles' ability to use words as guides for behaviour might be partly overcome. It was expected, therefore, that combined verbal-motor responses while showing no improvement over motor behaviour might show such an improvement if compared with verbal responses alone.

The results showed that the latter hypothesis, at least in so far as it concerns the rather complex experimental task, was untenable. A combination of verbal and motor responses gave no better results than either response modality alone when in the same modality as the stimulus. It seems that the use of motor movement does not reinforce a speech response, even when the motor system may be the relatively more intact. The motor responses obtained here, lacked the character of perceived voluntary movements and failed to facilitate stable joint activity of motor and speech behaviour even temporarily. An alternative inference from the results would be that the correct method of supporting a speech function has not been developed in this experiment.

The decisive factor enabling the subjects to comply partly with the instructions to respond in opposition to the direct signals, seems not to be the modality in which either stimulus or response is given. The tendencies to echolalia and echopraxia are more prominent if stimulus and response belong to the same modality. Cross modality reactions on the other hand seem to make a general instruction more effective, allowing greater mobility of response patterns. If the subject is required to tap when the experimenter is tapping, or to count when he is counting, the compelling force of the direct signal is too strong to permit any other than a purely imitative response. The subnormal subjects seem to remain stimulus bound. The impulses received from the stimuli do not generalize so readily if the subject is asked to respond in a different and not in a similar modality.

It was not too clear to us at this stage why this should be. It seemed possible that cross modality conditions necessitated translation from one type of sensory image to another. We therefore decided to investigate whether this process might prevent errors in recognition. The kind of errors we had in mind were caused by subjects simply saying "yes" indiscriminately when asked whether they had seen or heard the item before. While stereotyped affirmative responses of this kind would tend to be given to a series of pictures, substitution of the corresponding word in the recognition tests might favour discrimination.

To check the effect of the cross modality phenomenon we took short and long term memory into account, using visual and verbal signals (O'Connor and Hermelin 1961,a). Some subjects were shown pictures of everyday objects one by one, such as a tree or a cow, and asked some minutes later to recognize these pictures from among others of the same kind turned up one at a time. Other subjects heard a series of words which were the corresponding names of the pictures. After listening to these words they were asked to recognize them from among other words. The two groups of subjects thus went through the same procedure but one by sight and one by sound.

In keeping with the design of the previous experiment two more groups were used. One of these was a sight–sound group, the members of which saw the pictures, and in the recognition situation heard the words. The other was the sound–sight group, hearing the words and then identifying pictures. All the words were chosen from the vocabulary list developed by Mein (1961), selected from commonly used words by severely subnormal children. There were six subjects in each group. Eight items were presented on the first occasion and 16 in the recognition tests. Recognition tests were given shortly after the first presentation. A further group of 24 subjects was given the same recognition procedure after an interval of one week.

Cross modality effects appeared clearly in the results.

Analysis of variance established the difference between the two types of treatment, uni-modal and cross modal in both immediate and long term memory.

TABLE 14. MEAN TRANSFORMED RECOGNITION SCORES

	Immediate (N = 24)	Long term (N = 24)
Sound–Sound	9·0 ±9·7	8·5 ±12·2
Sight–Sight	17·0 ±21·9	1·3 ±3·2
Sound–Sight	31·1 ±24·3	18·4 ±18·8
Sight–Sound	43·9 ±23·8	19·8 ±21·2

Because of these results we formed the impression that a coding process might form the basis for the relative success under cross modal conditions. In our like modality trials we tended to get stereotyped affirmative responses, i.e. all words or all pictures were perceived as having occurred before. The necessity to translate verbal into visual stimuli and vice versa in the cross modality conditions may have made the association between words and images more specific.

If verbal encoding and decoding were responsible for the better results in the cross modality procedures, such methods would lose their effectiveness when the element of translation was absent.

In order to test this, Hermelin and O'Connor (1961,a), considered an operation in which verbal coding would become difficult and less likely. We selected the tactile exploration of complex non-representational shapes and compared that with visual inspection and recognition. The experiment has been mentioned before but we will consider it now in relation to the cross modality studies.

The subjects were again imbeciles and normal children of like mental age. The material consisted of 10 Russian and Greek letters. Only letters which differed as much as possible from any of the Roman alphabet were selected. The letters were cut out of brown hardboard, ⅛ in. thick, and were approximately 5 in. high. They were either inspected visually or they were manually explored when out of sight. Four matched subgroups of 15 normal and 4 of 15 subnormal children were formed, and four different treatments given. These were: (1) manual inspection of the stimulus figure and a stereognostic recognition test; (2) manual inspection and visual recognition; (3) visual inspection and visual recognition, and (4) visual inspection and stereognostic recognition.

The stimuli were presented successively for 10 sec each, with a time interval of 5 sec between stimuli. In the visual conditions they were placed on a light surface, on a table at about 18 in. distance from the subject's eyes. In the stereognostic conditions a screen 24 in. by 24 in., into which two openings had been cut, was placed on the table in front of the subject. The child put his hands through the two openings and the stimulus figure was put into them. According to the group to which the child was assigned, he was told either to look carefully at the figure or to explore it with his hands by feeling all around it. If necessary his hands were guided around the first figure. Immediately after five stimuli had been presented in this manner, recognition tests were given. In these the five inspection figures and five others were presented singly in succession in random order. Half the children from the manual inspection group were given stereognostic and half visual recognition tests. Similarly, half of those initially presented with five visual stimuli had to distinguish them from five others by manual exploration, while the remainder followed visual inspection with visual recognition tests. The subject was instructed to say whether or not he had seen or felt any particular figure on the previous occasion.

TABLE 15. MEAN RECOGNITION SCORES

	Stereog.–stereog.	Vision–vision	Stereog.–vision	Vision–stereog.
Imbecile	$31 \cdot 5 \pm 5 \cdot 7$	$19 \cdot 0 \pm 5 \cdot 9$	$19 \cdot 8 \pm 10 \cdot 9$	$19 \cdot 8 \pm 11 \cdot 8$
Normal	$22 \cdot 0 \pm 11 \cdot 9$	$26 \cdot 4 \pm 12 \cdot 2$	$24 \cdot 6 \pm 10 \cdot 6$	$19 \cdot 8 \pm 14 \cdot 3$

Recognition scores of normal children did not differ significantly between any of the four conditions. The children recognized the figures equally well whether they were visually or manually inspected, and like modality and cross modality trials gave the same results. The subnormal children showed a different pattern of results. Analysis of variance and subsequent "t" tests showed that while cross modality recognition trials did not differ from the visual like modality condition, tactile inspection and recognition resulted in a significantly better performance ($P = 0 \cdot 01$). Comparing the normal children with the imbeciles in an analysis of variance results in a significant interaction ($P = 0.025$) showing that the experimental conditions affect the groups differently. Subsequent "t" tests showed that while normals and subnormals do not differ from each other in cross modality recognition scores, the imbeciles are significantly better than normals in like modality stereognostic recognition ($P = 0.02$). The difference in visual recognition scores between the groups approaches but does not reach significance level.

We have suggested earlier that the relative success of the cross modality method, found in a previous experiment, may have been due to the element of verbal coding. Words were part of the material used, and the resulting necessity to encode verbal into visual and visual into verbal items may have made the stimuli more meaningful to the subject. Under those conditions recognition was aided.

The material used in the present experiment is not easily named, and in contrast with the previous study words were not among the items used. Under these circumstances it seemed that no translation from one type of sensory image into another took place and that the stimuli were not identified sufficiently in a one-trial presentation to be efficiently recognized by children whose level of mental development was below 7·7 years. This finding confirms the hypothesis stated earlier.

As far as imbeciles are concerned their impairment in visual discrimination has frequently been noted. It seems that shape discrimination in this modality does not develop beyond the mental age-level of about 5 years. The present experiment suggests, however, that, in some imbeciles at least, development of stereognosis may not be equally impaired or arrested. If this finding is supported in further experiments, implications for alternative teaching methods of imbecile children should be considered.

What is relevant to the present discussion, however, is the fact that as long as verbal coding is an inherent part of the task severely subnormal subjects attain higher levels of efficiency than when such coding is absent. As the reversal experiment and the cross modality studies have shown, responses become more stable and specific when connections between words and direct stimuli are built up. Without this coding element, responses remain on a more primitive level. It is this bond between the verbal system and motor behaviour, between stimuli and their appropriate code, which is insufficiently developed in the subnormals. The translation of stimuli from one modality into another without changing their meaning must be emphasized in the presentation of problems for the severely subnormal subject.

Concluding, these results indicate:

1. While "like modality" stimulus response conditions lead to stereotyped, echolalic behaviour and leave the subject stimulus bound, "cross modality" conditions allow greater mobility of response pattern.
2. The necessity for verbal coding in the translation of stimuli from one modality to another seems to be a contributory factor for better achievement.
3. In conditions in which verbal coding is difficult the cross modality method loses its effectiveness.

CHAPTER VII

RECALL AND RECOGNITION

EXTENSIVE experimental evidence on normal subjects is available on quantitative and qualitative aspects of memory, as well as on the nature of the storing mechanism. Few of the findings, however, have ever been systematically tested with defectives. There are, of course, many observations in the literature which are concerned with the memory of the subnormal. Tredgold (1952) observes that:

> Retentiveness, or the tenacity of memory, does not seem to differ greatly in the majority of defectives from the normal. But the readiness with which experiences can be recalled is usually inferior, as would be expected from their limited range of interests, poor understanding and defective attention.
>
> Defect of recall is characteristic of so many aments that, like attention, it has been held to be the prime cause of their condition. But I cannot agree with this view. There are many aments whose memory, far from being defective, is really extraordinary, as we shall see in describing idiots savants; and the defective child can often remember isolated happenings, which have impressed him at the time, quite as long and as faithfully as can the normal. Dr. E. O. Lewis, as a result of some special observations on the subject, came to the conclusion that the memory of defectives was inferior to that of normal persons, primarily because of its poverty of rational associations; I think there is no doubt that this is true, and that the defective's memory of events is much more often a consequence than a cause of their general imperfection of mind. The defective child does not register and therefore cannot retain things, because he is not interested in them; or he does not understand, and consequently does not attend to them. (Pp. 93–94.)

Tredgold also quotes case histories of patients in mental deficiency institutions who have outstanding calculating or memory abilities. Such persons, of whom there may be one or two in a hospital, show capacities of recall in certain limited fields which appear to be outside the capacities of normal adults.

True, normal adults store in their minds a multitude of facts which they think little of, and these may amount to more than the special scope of the idiot-savant. However, the development of the mind even in one direction in an imbecile is remarkable enough to demand further investigation. This remains to be done.

Ingham (1952), in his studies of recognition, concludes that a relationship of a limited kind existed between memory capacity and intelligence, but he would not regard this as generalizable to all materials or all levels of intelligence. Sarason (1953) points out that of the 20 items in the Binet test, in which according to Thompson and Magaret (1947) normals surpassed defectives, eight involved memory. He concludes however, that as fear and anxiety adversely affect performance on memory items, such items cannot be relied upon as a valid indication of intellectual capacity. It is therefore uncertain whether memory follows a normal or an abnormal pattern in imbeciles. E. O. Lewis, as quoted by Tredgold, makes the point that defectives may not recall so well because they fail to record. The question remains, however, whether they remember *what* they record.

We have dealt with a few aspects of the memory process which seemed particularly relevant as far as subnormals were concerned. No doubt there are other characteristics of recall and recognition, which we have so far ignored. Thus any possible qualitative difference between short and long term memory has not been investigated, nor have qualitative changes in memorized material had sufficient attention.

Amongst the most relevant memory studies for our purpose are those which deal with the effect of meaningfulness of material on recognition and recall. The level of retention curves as a function of meaningfulness of material was brought out clearly by Davis and Moore (1935). Often the degree of meaningfulness of material is closely related with the subject's ability to name it. Language and its relation to memory, learning and recognition is of such importance in the thought problems of the subnormals that it has been discussed separately at length. With normals, in cases of verbal learning a large quantity of material is better remembered than a small quantity learned to the same criterion (Hovland, 1938). This is probably due to the greater amount of practice required to learn the larger amount. If it is true that the more trials needed to learn the more is retained, this may have interesting implications for recall in subnormals. However, the degree of learning is of course also relevant for memory, and superior retention with higher degree of learning has clearly been shown (Krueger, 1929). The amount of material which, once learned, can be retained is probably of crucial importance for the learning ability of subnormals.

One characteristic of the material determining the amount recalled is its vividness. Von Restorff (1933) and later Pillsbury and Raush (1943) showed that items which are in some way different or isolated from the rest of the material will be better remembered. Obviously vividness serves as a focus for attention. The focusing of attention is one of the processes held by us to be impaired in defectives. Consequently presenting material in such a way that attention to its relevant features is facilitated may help subnormals in their learning and memory.

Thus we are left with some theoretically interesting suggestions which need to be investigated. These concern the relationship between the amount learned and the amount recalled; the degree of learning and the nature or size of the storing mechanism. Another subject which arises from our own work concerns the mental age at which learning of material takes place. Our results suggest that this might be very relevant to its recall. It could conceivably be related to those findings described above which show that the meaningfulness of material aids in its recall.

We planned and carried out recall experiments which follow those which have been described in previous chapters. These, it will be remembered, indicated that an encoding process seemed to facilitate recognition. This may reflect the value of "meaningfulness" as an aid to recall or rather show the importance of verbal formulation in this respect.

The experiment which is now to be described followed observations showing the presence of long term retention of both motor and symbolic material by imbeciles. In one of our experiments not previously reported, average learning scores on recognition of printed words were reduced from a first learning score averaging 4·5 trials to a relearning score of 0·3 trials after three months without rehearsal. In the cross modality experiments discussed, partial recognition of material over a period of 14 days was shown.

As has been mentioned, probably one of the most decisive questions about limits of learning capacity in imbecile children is the relationship between how much they can learn at any one time, and how much of what they learned they can remember.

Experimental evidence from normals has shown that there is a difference between the span of absolute judgement and the span of immediate memory. Judgement in Miller's (1956) sense of the word is a function of the amount of information contained in the stimulus situation, or of the number of other possible alternatives. The limiting factor in identifying a stimulus is the size of the set of alternatives from which the stimuli are drawn. In other words, absolute judgement is a limit on the amount of information which the observer can extract from the stimuli.

The span of immediate memory is a limit on the items that can be recalled and is independent of the amount of information represented in each item. This last generalization seems also to hold for the result of experiments which are scored according to repeated trials.

Brogden and Smith (1954) used verbal mazes with either 16 or 24 choice points, and the number of alternatives per choice point varied, so that some mazes had 2, others 3, 4 and up to 12 alternatives at every choice point. Subjects practised until they achieved one perfect repetition. It was found that the number of trials needed to learn a maze was independent of the number of alternatives at the choice points. In other words the difficulty in remembering a sequence of verbal items depended on the length of the sequence and not on the possible alternatives. It was independent of the amount of information represented in each item.

However, an important qualification is that these results hold only if trials are used as a measure of learning. If instead the number of errors are scored, there is an increase as the number of alternatives increases. So learning does seem to become more difficult with an increase in alternatives, but once a correct response is made it is repeated as easily as one which has had a smaller number of alternatives. In our experiment single stimuli, in this case capital letters, had to be identified from amongst different numbers of alternative letters. These letters were presented with either 2, 3, 6 or 10 alternative ones. Number of trials to learn to identify one particular letter was scored for each level of complexity. Immediate memory for four letters was compared with immediate memory for eight letters. According to Miller's (1956) findings mentioned before, the amount remembered in this case should be independent of the number of alternatives with which each letter was formerly presented. Instead it should depend on the limits of the memory span. Finally, long term was compared with immediate memory.

The subjects were 12 institutionalized imbecile children, I.Q. 30–36, mean I.Q. 33·6, aged from 9 to 15 years. None of the children had at any time attended reading classes in the occupation centre of the institution. A complete alphabet of plastic capital letters was used. Each letter was 25 mm high. As 29 stimuli were needed for the experiment, three letters from the lower case alphabet, equal in height and material to the capitals were included.

The experiment was carried out in five stages, which will be described separately:

(a) Four single letters had to be identified, and each one was presented together with a different number of alternative letters.

(b) An immediate memory test was given.

(c) Four further letters were learned, presented at the same levels of choice complexity as the first four.

(d) An immediate memory test for all eight letters was given.

(e) After a week's time interval memory for all eight letters was retested.

The first four letters which had to be identified were K, B, E and S. Each of these was presented in turn to each subject individually. Each letter was presented together with other, alternative ones, the number of other alternatives being 2, 3, 6 and 10. Order of presentation of letters and of complexity level, were varied according to a Graeco-Latin square design. Each subject was presented with each letter in a different order of choice complexity. Thus three variables could be compared: relative difficulty of learning a particular letter, number of trials needed to learn on each level of choice complexity and effect of order of presentation.

In order to ensure that the subjects did not know the letters prior to the experiment each was asked before the first session, "Can you pick out K? (or B, E, S)". If the subject was able to do this he was excluded from the experiment; otherwise the correct letter was pointed out to him. The letters were then rearranged on a tray, re-presented, and the subject was asked again: "Which one is K?" Each correct choice was rewarded and each incorrect one corrected. After each trial the position of the letters was rearranged, and after four consecutive correct responses had been given the next set of letters was presented.

Immediately after the four letters had been learned up to cri-

TABLE 16. LETTER DISCRIMINATION

LETTERS

	First four letters					Second four letters				
	K	B	E	S	Total	R	F	A	U	Total
Mean for 12 subjects	2·3	2·7	3·1	2·1	10·2	1·2	1·5	1·6	1·5	5·8

ORDER

	First four letters					Second four letters				
	I	II	III	IV	Total	I	II	III	IV	Total
Mean for 12 subjects	3·0	1·9	3·2	2·1	10·2	1·6	1·5	1·4	1·3	5·8

COMPLEXITY

	First four letters					Second four letters				
	Number of other alternatives					Number of other alternatives				
	2	3	6	10	Total	2	3	6	10	Total
Mean for 12 subjects	2·0	2·3	2·7	3·2	10·2	1·3	1·2	1·3	2·0	5·8

terion they were re-presented in the same order in which they had first been learned. Each one was, however, presented with all 21 previously used alternative letters. Thus information content was presumably increased. However, there was also some redundancy, as 21 letters had already been identified as *not* being K, B, E and S. If the findings from normals were applicable for imbecile children, the rise in complexity level in the form of an increased number of alternatives should be without effect on immediate memory. Other questions asked were: Would the amount of information initially contained in the stimulus display affect memory differentially? Would some particular letters be better remembered than others? Would the order in which the letters were learned have any effect on remembering them?

The result of the discrimination learning can be seen in the above table. As this shows, learning was very quick in all instances, many subjects needing only one trial and none more than nine to identify any one letter correctly. The mean total number of trials for the subjects to learn all four letters was 10·2, with a range from 4 to 23. This represents a mean of 2·55 trials per letter, rather faster discrimination learning than is usually found in imbecile children. It is possible, though not very likely, that this was a particularly easy perceptual discrimination task. A more probable and realistic explanation is that incidental and latent learning in letter identification occurred prior to the experiment. Though not formally taught, even institutionalized imbecile children cannot fail to get into contact with much printed material in the form of comics, television titles, etc.

TABLE 17. IMMEDIATE MEMORY

	Four letters	Eight letters		
		First four	Second four	Eight letters
	Number remembered	Number remembered	Number remembered	Number remembered
Mean of 12 subjects	3·1	2·3	1·9	4·2

The number of trials needed to learn did not differ significantly between particular letters or order of presentation. However, a consistent and significant increase in number of trials needed to learn to criterion is apparent as the number of possible alternatives increases.

Scores for the memory tests are given in the Immediate Memory table. Neither letters, orders nor initial complexity seem to have had any differential effect. Out of a possible 4 a mean of 3·1 letters is remembered. Eight out of 12 children remembered all four letters and two remembered none.

At the next stage the same procedure, which has been described, was repeated using four new letters as stimuli to be identified. These had not appeared before as either correct or incorrect stimuli. The four new letters were R, F, A and U. The four previously identified letters K, B, E and S were not used as either correct or incorrect stimuli. Following this, each of the eight letters learned had to be re-identified, in the same order in which it had originally been learned. Each one in turn was presented together with the 21 alternative letters.

Finally, after a seven-day interval, recognition tests for the eight letters were repeated. On all memory tests a single trial only was allowed. No corrections were given, but the correct choices were rewarded.

The results of this part of the experiment are interesting because there was a considerable reduction in trials to learn the second four as compared with the first four letters. A mean total of 5·8 as compared with 10·2 trials for four letters, or a mean of 1·5 against 2·5 trials for a single letter was needed. There are no obvious reasons to suppose R, F, A and U are easier to learn than K, B, E and S, although it would have been better to have each half of a subgroup learn each set of letters first. All the same it seems fairly safe to conclude that learning sets are at least partly responsible for the reduced number of trials in the second discrimination task. As can be seen from the table, the scores continue to decrease consistently in this set of letters according to order of presentation.

Another possible explanation for the decrease in trials is that all 21 alternative letters had already appeared before, while R, F, A and U were presented for the first time in this task. Discrimination might have taken place according to the one new stimulus in each display. According to this, one would have to suppose that along with the previous positive four stimuli, the 21 alternative ones had also been learned, at least to such a degree that a new, not previously seen letter stood out. As the reduction in trials becomes marked only at this stage and not during the learning of the first set of four letters there is at least some support for such a supposition. No marked difference in scores was found for displays containing 2, 3 and 6 other alternatives respectively. Discrimination from 10 other alternatives seems considerably more difficult, and the number of trials needed increased significantly.

As can be seen from the last table there was a relative loss in retention on the second memory task when compared with the first. Only half, or 4·2 out of eight letters, could be re-identified. The score of the first four dropped from 3·1 to 2·3 and out of the second four letters only 1·9 were retained. If any two letters from the first and second four are compared, either according to complexity level or according to order of presentation, those learned earlier are remembered better. It is probably relevant that these first four had already been recalled once before, and that in addition they had originally taken longer to acquire. Thus material learned earlier in a sequence seems better remembered. In addition a relationship between number of initial presentations and recall is suggested by the results.

Subjects remembered the eight letters better after a time interval of seven days than they had immediately after learning. Three subjects, who made no score on the immediate memory test, were able to remember after a time interval. The interesting point, however, is that the rise in scores is solely due to a recovery in the memory for the first four letters. A mean of 3·1, identical with the one before the second discrimination task was presented, is achieved by the subjects. Memory scores for the second set of four letters learned remain low, 1·7 against 1·9 on the immediate testing. No consistent effects from initial level of complexity or order of presentation within each set of four letters are evident in the memory task.

Several different implications of the results must be considered. One is whether discrimination and memory of stimuli, presented together with a varying number of alternative stimuli, is subject to the same laws which have been suggested to operate in normals. Another is the relationship of long term and short term memory.

One point which should be stressed again is the fast learning in this discrimination task, which suggests that some incidental learning to identify letters had taken place prior to the experiment. The capacity for such latent and incidental learning, which is also evident in the ability of such subjects to transfer and build up learning sets, is an important asset to be taken into account in the teaching of imbecile children.

As in normals, perceptual discrimination learning is a function of the number of alternatives from which the stimulus has to be drawn. It needs more trials to identify a letter from a display containing 11 alternatives than from one with 3 alternatives. This again has obvious practical implications for teaching methods.

As far as memory is concerned, learning of additional material interferes with the retention of that first learned. This is well in line with results from normals. However, this interference seems to wear off after a time interval and no loss on long term memory over initial remembering is apparent with the material presented on a first discrimination task. A second set of letters is remembered equally badly under both conditions. Whether that is due to a limit to the amount of material that can be retained, or whether it is a function of the number of trials needed to learn, is not clear from this experiment. Concluding, it seems that the processing and retention of information of imbecile children is not qualitatively different from that of normals. As in Brogden and Smith's (1954) experiment mentioned earlier, the number of errors in identification increases as the number of alternatives increases. Once learned, the number of elements remembered is independent of the amount of information represented in each item, but seems to depend on the length of the sequence. In addition, in this experiment with imbecile children, which element is remembered and which is not, depends on its original position in such a sequence.

An indication that the amount recalled is not always a function of the initial number of trials needed to learn is given in the experiment on variation of letter size which was mentioned earlier. In this experiment a control and an experimental group differed significantly in the number of trials they needed to identify printed words. However, in a subsequent memory test, there was no significant difference between the groups, both remembering equally well. It seemed that degree of initial learning did affect memory, whereas the number of trials it took to reach a criterion of proficiency did not.

A distinction must, however, be made between number of trials it takes to learn, and number of repetitions of presentation. If, as House and Zeaman (1960,b) suggest, many trials may pass before the learning curves of defectives show any rise, subnormals may need more trials before true learning commences. House and Zeaman think that impaired attention may be responsible for this.

Alternatively, Guggenbuel as early as 1840 suggested that raising the intensity level of the stimulus may help the defective to focus his attention on it. Sheridan (personal communication) stresses the importance of an adequately high level of intensity of sound stimuli for language development in young normal children. Thus in the following experiment O'Connor and Hermelin (1962) attempted to test the relative effects on recall of frequency and intensity of stimulus presentation.

A further hypothesis was examined. This concerned types of word associations which are given more frequently by adults and children respectively. One may assume that the ease of learning to give one word as a response to another would be a function of the strength of association between them. This was taken into account in planning the experiment.

Two sets of six word pairs were given to two groups, an imbecile group (N = 40) and a normal group (N = 40) of approximately the same mental age. The children were 6-year-olds in the first two classes of an infant school and the imbeciles were adult patients in a mental deficiency hospital. The average age of the patients was 22 with a range from 15 to 35. Their mean I.Q. was 46·4 with a range from 40 to 57. The word imbecile is therefore used loosely to cover this range. However, only three of the severely subnormal subjects had I.Q.s in excess of 50. The subnormals were clinically heterogeneous, and only those with any hearing defects were excluded.

Subnormals and normals were each randomly allocated to one of four sub-groups of 10 subjects each. The task was the learning of words presented as paired associates. Two different sets of words were used alternatively, half the subjects being presented with *List A* and half with *List B*. The stimulus words in each list are the same, and the associates are the most frequently given spontaneous response words for children and adults respectively. The words are taken from Woodworth (1946) and are shown in the table.

TABLE 18. WORD LISTS USED IN LEARNING AND RECALL

List A	List B
Stimulus–Response	Stimulus–Response
Dark–night	Mountain–hill
Man–work	Man–woman
Table–eat	Soft–hard
Deep–hole	Table–chair
Soft–pillow	Deep–shallow
Mountain–high	Dark–light

Four treatments were given:

(1) Low intensity of sound presentation and fewer repetitions.
(2) Low intensity of sound presentation and many repetitions.
(3) High intensity of sound presentation and fewer repetitions.
(4) High intensity of sound presentation and many repetitions.

Number of trials and level of sound intensity are given in the next table.

The words were recorded on magnetic tape and presented through a loud speaker. A Dawe sound meter was used to determine the appropriate distance of the subject from the noise source at which the stimuli would be received at the specified intensities. The level of background noise in the experimental rooms was approximately 40–45 dB, as measured by the Dawe meter. Subjects were seen individually. They were told in advance that they would hear some words, two at a time, that word pairs belonged together and that they would hear them many times to help them to remember them.

In the learning session both stimulus and response words were read out. In recall sessions only stimulus words were given and subjects were asked to give the appropriate response. There were three response sessions which occurred: (i) after one minute, (ii) after two days, (iii) after one month. It is possible to regard the first as a measure of learning or of immediate recall, while responses given after two days and one month can be regarded as short and long term recall respectively.

Mean scores for each group of ten subjects out of a possible six are set out in the table.

TABLE 19. MEAN SCORES BY GROUPS AND OCCASIONS

Bd	Repetitions	Normals			Imbeciles		
		1 min	2 days	1 month	1 min	2 days	1 month
55	10	4·3	4·5	4·4	4·0	4·2	4·2
	20	5·1	5·1	5·0	4·9	4·9	4·4
90	10	4·5	5·0	5·3	4·5	4·3	3·9
	20	5·0	5·2	5·5	5·5	5·4	5·4

In separate analyses for each occasion, it was found that at no time did the different word lists *A* and *B* show a significant effect on the scores. Therefore the data over lists was combined for a further analysis of mixed design over groups, treatment and occasions. There was no significant difference between scores of normals and subnormals on any of the occasions or under any treatment. There was also no statistically significant difference between the groups for the number of items they recalled on any of the occasions. However, a trend in the data, although not to a significant extent, was a tendency for an increase over time in the scores of the normals, and a corresponding decrease for the imbeciles. This tendency might well have become more marked if memory had been tested over a longer period of time. The analysis showed a highly significant treatment difference in immediate as well as short and long term recall. This difference was most marked when a presentation of 90 dB intensity and 20 trials was compared with one of 55 dB and 10 trials. However, even with intensity level held constant at either 90 dB or 55 dB, those subjects who had 20 presentations had significantly higher scores than those with 10 presentations. Keeping the number of presentations constant while varying intensity level has no significant effect. But under conditions of 90 dB intensity and 10 trials, and 55 dB and 20 trials the scores do not differ significantly. These last findings suggest that, though frequency of presentation determines the amount immediately recalled, intensity level also appears to contribute. Many presentations at a lower intensity level give no significantly better results than fewer at a higher intensity, and the most favourable conditions are those under which the material is presented many times at a high intensity level.

Thus, in this experiment there was no significant difference in learning or memory scores between normals and imbeciles of like mental age. Frequency of presentation affected immediate recall scores of both groups with intensity level contributing to a lesser degree. However, these variables affect immediate recall or learning rather than memory over a longer time interval. Those who were presented with the material less often retained as much of what they initially recalled as did those who had more frequent presentation.

Though the two sets of response words differed in the frequency with which they were associated with the stimulus words, the more frequent were neither easier to learn nor better remembered than the less frequent. A similar failure to obtain differences in ease of paired associate learning as a function of the frequency of association has been reported by Haun (1960). Haun concludes that free association is not only a function of the strength of association between words but also of various uncontrolled factors such as familiarity of usage, set, etc. Thus failure of recall should not imply lack of association.

Certain practical and intriguing inferences may be made from the data. One important conclusion from these experiments is that if material has been learned up to the same criterion, it is irrelevant for memory how many trials it took to obtain this criterion. If, on the other hand, frequency of presentation has an effect on learning scores, then this effect is maintained in the level of recall efficiency.

The results presented are evidence that learning if pursued to a sufficiently exacting criterion may be relatively permanent in imbe-

ciles. These conditions are best achieved by frequent presentations
of the material to be learned at high intensity.

The conclusions from the experiments on memory of the severely
subnormal could be stated as follows:

1. While visual discrimination learning in imbeciles is a function
   of the amount of information contained in the stimuli, memory
   is independent of the amount of information represented in
   each item.
2. Learning of new material at first interferes with remembering
   previously learned items, but this interference is of short
   duration only.
3. There is a limit to the amount remembered after massed trial
   learning. Which item is remembered and which not depends
   on its original position in the sequence.
4. Two groups of imbeciles needing different numbers of trials
   to learn to the same criterion remember equally well. It seems
   that it is the degree of initial learning which determines memory,
   whereas the number of trials it took to reach a criterion of
   proficiency does not.
5. Under all the learning conditions, in which meaningfully
   paired associates are presented in our experiment, imbeciles
   remember as well as normals of like mental age.
6. Frequency of presentations affects normals and subnormals
   equally, and this effect is more evident in learning than in long
   term recall.

CHAPTER VIII

MONGOLS AND OTHER IMBECILES

PART of our programme for research included the differentiation of sub-types of mental deficiency in terms of measurable behaviour characteristics. We are able to offer only limited conclusions in this field because we have made very few investigations. Clinicians have noted the high average age of the mothers of mongol children. Penrose (1949) suggested that this was about 37 years, compared with the mothers of normal children which is about 29 years. The mongols' expectation of life is about nine years and many are stillborn or do not survive the first year. Carter (1958) states that two-thirds are dead by the age of 12.

More recently considerable interest has been aroused by chromosomal studies of mongols. Chromosomal anomalies are present in all mongols. This has supported the hypothesis of common personality traits in this group. However, chromosomal abnormalities may not result in characteristic personality changes, but may leave the personality free to manifest a wide range of qualities. It may be the case that finer analysis of chromosomal structure would reveal the source of individual differences but in our opinion such an hypothesis remains to be established. This does not, of course, prevent us making attempts to establish differences in behaviour patterns between mongols and other imbeciles. This we have attempted to do without trying to determine whether or no such differences have a genetic basis.

A review of the literature shows that whilst specific physiological characteristics have been attributed to mongols and generally agreed, this is not true of psychological patterns. Many studies have made this clear but especially those of Rollin (1946) and Blacketer-Simmonds (1953). These call in question the supposedly genial, friendly and music loving qualities of the mongol personality. Such clinical assumptions had held sway for a long time in medical practice and it is interesting to hear the opposition to the acceptance of the pattern so many years after the syndrome was first described by Langdon-Down in 1866.

Few psychological studies of mongols have been made but Gordon (1944) compared mongol and normal children on visual and tactile discrimination for size, shape and texture. He found no differences in the visual tasks but the normals had significantly better tactile discrimination. The only example of a study consciously planned to differentiate mongols from other imbeciles apart from the experiments described below is that of Lyle (1959, 1960). This was concerned with the effect of an institution environment on the verbal development of imbecile children. Results suggested that the restrictive environment of some hospitals had a deleterious effect on verbal development in imbeciles, and that this affected mongols more seriously than it did non-mongols. In more favourable environmental conditions mongols and imbeciles were of equal verbal intelligence, while there was a nine months difference in the institutionalized group.

Our own approach was an attempt to collect data elucidating the relationship between psychological and physiological response patterns. There are two procedures used by psychologists to assess "psycho-physiological" activity, and work of this kind with the subnormal has recently been reviewed by Berkson (1961). Firstly, basal or resting levels can be measured, in which no special stimuli are presented. Characteristically during such a procedure skin conductance readings decrease over time. The second procedure involves measuring the degree of response to short duration stimuli. The response is usually a change in the psychophysiological readings, occurring within three seconds after the onset of the stimulus. There is usually a decrement of response intensity over trials.

Some investigations have dealt with comparing basic physiological levels of normals and subnormals, but few have tried to differentiate patients within the defective group. O'Connor and Venables (1956) found skin conductance in imbeciles to be higher than in normals. Even within the imbeciles group a negative correlation between I.Q. and conductance was found. Ellis and Sloan (1957) confirmed the difference in conductance between normals and defectives but failed to find a consistent relationship of intellectual and conductance level within the subnormal group. Another contradictory finding is that of Collman (1931, 1959) who found mentally deficient children to have not higher but lower skin conductance than normal children. In view of this we thought it necessary to repeat the investigation of basic level of skin conductance, using normal, feebleminded, non-mongol imbecile and mongol imbecile subjects (Berkson, Hermelin and O'Connor, 1961). Two other measures of resting levels were also taken. One was the number of heartbeats in a one minute period, and the other was the alpha index, i.e. the percentage of the presence of alpha waves in the E.E.G. record within a predetermined time interval.

Neither of these last two measures distinguished between the groups. There was, however, a significant group difference in the amount of skin conductance. The imbeciles had the highest skin conductance, followed by the feebleminded and the normals. This was consistent with previous results of O'Connor and Venables (1956). An additional result was, however, that the mongols showed a lower conductance level than the other subnormal groups. In fact their readings were similar to those obtained from normals.

TABLE 20. SKIN CONDUCTANCE IN MICROMHOS

	N	Initial measure	Intermediate measure	Final measure
Imbeciles	19	26	25	23
Feebleminded	18	24	22	21
Normals	16	20	19	18
Mongol imbeciles	17	19	17	15

The results presented in this table are clearcut so far as the first three groups are concerned. Decrease of intelligence shows an increase of conductance in all three columns but the mongol results do not follow this pattern. The investigation by O'Connor and Venables did not include more than one or two mongol imbeciles whose scores were swamped in the group.

J. H. Clark, in an unpublished study, repeated our experiment using groups of mongol children and adults and non-mongol imbecile children and adults. Irrespective of sex and age and with a sample carefully matched for I.Q., he was able to confirm our finding. The next table shows conductance scores in micromhos. The mongols have lower skin conductance than the other imbeciles.

TABLE 21. SKIN CONDUCTANCE IN MICROMHOS

	Adults		Children	
	Male	Female	Male	Female
Mongol imbeciles	9·5	9·8	7·6	6·6
Non-mongol imbeciles	13·3	11·4	8·5	8·5

Analysis of variance and 't' testing of these results show that mongols and non-mongols differ significantly in conductance and that in addition adults and children differ significantly. It is to be noted that the conductance scores of adults are higher than those of children.

In a number of studies concerned with parameters of the alpha rhythm, the conclusions have usually been that comparison of normals and mentally deficient adults shows no differences between their mean alpha frequencies (Berkson, 1961). Two studies have compared normal and subnormal patients in the blocking of the alpha rhythm. Lindsley and Berkson, in an unpublished study reported the duration of alpha blocking after a light flash to be significantly shorter in feebleminded than in normal subjects. In our investigation (Berkson, Hermelin and O'Connor, 1961) the stimuli were a series of light flashes administered while the subject was lying in an otherwise dark quiet room. Duration of alpha blocking was taken as a response measure to the flashes.

The criterion for measuring alpha return was the beginning of a burst of at least five alpha waves, one of which was at least 50 per cent of the height of the tallest wave in the one second prior to the light flash. The within group variances of alpha block data were markedly heterogeneous and non-parametric tests were used in the analysis. The normals showed a significantly longer alpha block than did the combined subnormal group. There was no difference within the defective groups on any of the measures of response amplitude or duration following the presentation of simple stimuli.

Change in skin potential was also measured after the light flashes. The amplitude of the skin potential change was determined by measuring from the base-line to the peak of the psychogalvanic response, employing either negative or positive deflection or a sum of the base to peak heights if both were present. The analysis of variance showed a significant difference between the groups in response to the first stimulus. The normals showed significantly more potential change than the defectives but the latter did not differ significantly amongst themselves.

Though no differences between mongol and non-mongol imbeciles could be established in alpha-blocking time and skin potential change such differences are shown in other measures. Thus mongols showed a greater amount of eye movement in various conditions than did non-mongols of the same intelligence level, when the lateral and vertical eye movements of subjects were measured by O'Connor and Berkson in an unpublished study.

In addition to a completely dark field there were two static displays, a field illuminated by one bulb of intensity approximately 110 ft lamberts placed centrally 15 in. in front of the subject's head, and a second condition in which five lights of total intensity 110 ft lamberts were arranged in a semi-circle 15 in. from the subject. There were two changing displays corresponding to the two static displays. In the first, one light flashed intermittently at intervals of between 5 and 10 sec. staying on for ½ sec., and in the second the five lights were presented in random order using the same intervals.

The subject sat in a dark room with his chin resting on a chin rest in a metal frame. The frame supported a sectioned cardboard drum of 2 ft 6 in. diameter painted matt black in which the horizontal semi-circle of five lights was arranged. The subject's head was 15 in. from all points on this curved surface. Lights were at eye level and 6 in. apart covering a distance of 24 in. and subtending an angle of approximately 90 degrees at the subject's eyes.

Each of the subjects was presented with the five chosen displays in random order taking three minutes over each display. Eye movements and eye blinks were measured, using an electro-oculographic technique similar to that described by Marg (1951) in his review of the literature and further developed by Shackel (1960). This technique involved the fitting of electrodes to the forehead and the cheek above and below one eye. Two further electrodes were fitted, one to the right of the right eye and one to the left of the left eye. Vertical movements or blinks and lateral movements respectively were thus measurable. An AC amplifier was used. As a result of the use of this type of instrument only a recording of the total amount of eye movements could be made and not a recording of different positions of the eyes. An earth was attached to the scalp.

Nurses served as controls in this experiment and were matched in age with the defectives, being between 18 and 32 years old. The average ages for the groups were 24 and 26·2 years. The I.Q. of the two imbecile groups was matched, averaging between 32 and 33 points of I.Q. for each group. Each group was composed of 14 subjects.

The data consist of summated eye movements under different conditions of illumination and changes in amount of eye movement from one condition to another. We are concerned here only with mongol-imbecile differences. Total eye movement according to each lighting condition is presented as a group average in the following table.

TABLE 22. MEAN EYE MOVEMENTS OF THREE SUBJECT GROUPS UNDER FIVE CONDITIONS OF ILLUMINATION

	Darkness	One flashing light	Five flashing lights	One steady light	Five steady lights
Normals (N = 14)	124·38 ±21·20	124·24 ±13·64	128·66 ±21·15	130·95 ±28·69	141·02 ±33·78
Non-mongol imbeciles (N = 14)	122·88 ±15·87	124·74 ±15·08	125·74 ±13·04	131·30 ±15·14	136·52 ±17·33
Mongol imbeciles (N = 14)	148·51 ±16·66	150·23 ±19·92	153·51 ±20·22	168·22 ±22·68	173·22 ±29·57

Analysis of variance of these results showed overall group differences for all conditions significant at a level less than 0·001. The interaction between groups and conditions was not significant and the overall analysis of variance between conditions was significant at less than the 0·001 level.

Thus, while increase in illumination increases lateral saccadic eye movements irrespective of subgroup examined, it is also clear that the eye movement scores of mongol imbeciles are much greater than those of either normals or non-mongol imbeciles.

However, it could not be inferred directly and with certainty that eye movements are more frequent in mongols. It might have been the case that eyeball potentials were greater in mongols. If this were so the same amount of movement of the eye might result in a higher potential score which would appear as more movement if the record were interpreted directly. This has been shown not to be the case. Norris (personal communication) has shown that the eyeball potential of mongols does not differ significantly from that of non-mongol imbeciles.

Turning from psychological measures to those of motor speed, motor control and sensitivity, we have to re-examine some of the previously mentioned experimental results. Thus in the series of reaction time experiments mentioned before Berkson (1960 a, b and c) found mongols significantly slower than non-mongols. O'Connor and Hermelin (1961,b) found that mongols had a much poorer tactile discrimination ability than other non-mongol imbeciles of the same age and I.Q. While non-mongol imbeciles obtained higher stereognostic recognition scores than normals of like mental age, those of the mongols were much lower.

We also (Hermelin and O'Connor 1961,b) found that while no difference in visual discrimination and recognition of shapes was apparent, the mongols were worse than other imbeciles in copying and reproducing designs.

In conclusion, we would like to offer some suggestions for possible underlying mechanisms which would account for the functional differences which we observed.

Experimental results from normals show that reaction time as well as skin resistance are associated with muscle tone. Davis (1940) has shown that the greater the tension level in the responding muscle systems, the shorter the reaction time. Kennedy and

Travis (1947) also found that lowered muscular tension produced longer reaction times. Thus if impairment of the cerebellum would lead to hypotonia in mongols, their slower reaction time responses might be attributed to the lack of muscular tension. Likewise, Freeman and Simpson (1938) have shown that there is a decrease in skin resistance under increased muscular tension. This seems to indicate that the high skin resistance found in mongols may also be due to their lack of muscle tone. That hypotonia would minimize kinesthetic feedback and thus impair stereognosis seems plausible, and as suggested before even the large amount of eye movement in the mongols could possible be due to hypotonia, although this needs more investigation. Lack of muscle tone, of course, indicates a low state of arousal. However, the precise nature of this association and the causal relationships involved are complex.

Alternatively the low skin conductance and poor stereognosis of the mongols may have been the function of some peripheral characteristic such as the coarseness, thickness and dryness of their skin.

Arousal is held to be a function of the non-specific subcortical systems, and recent research reviewed by Ina Samuels (1959) suggests that these systems may not be quite as non-specific as has been assumed. Bernhaut, Gellhorn and Rasmussen (1953) have shown that proprioceptive stimuli are more effective in arousing an animal from a light anaesthetic state than are visual stimuli, and while this may be true of the non-mongol imbeciles, in mongols the cortical and/or subcortical systems concerned with muscular or skin sensitivity may be in a state of inhibition. On the other hand, visual stimuli seem to alert mongols as much as they do non-mongols, though both groups are less responsive to such stimuli than are normals. This suggestion finds additional confirmation in the fact that the duration of alpha blocking after light stimuli was the same for mongols as for other defective groups, while the normals had longer blocking times before the alpha returned.

When talking about perception we mentioned differences between mongol and non-mongol imbeciles in stereognostic and drawing ability. The mongols gave a significantly poorer performance in both tasks.

H

The upshot of this research is, therefore, that we can make some claim to have shown some ways in which mongols differ from imbeciles of the same I.Q., each one possibly due to a common mechanism. To this extent we think that we have prised loose the grip which the I.Q. has had on investigations in this field.

We hope in addition that we have given an example of an attempt to relate psychological and physiological functions. We very much appreciate the penalties for false moves in such an endeavour and for this reason we advance our explanatory hypothesis with some caution, but we consider that it is worth while to attempt such a liaison.

Finally, the result from these experiments can be summarized as follows:

1. Under conditions of minimal stimulation, mongols have a lower basic level of skin conductance than non-mongols of the same I.Q.
2. Various physiological measures of response to short duration stimuli distinguish between normals and defectives, but do not result in significant differences within the defective groups.
3. Mongols show a greater amount of eye movement in various conditions of illumination than non-mongols.
4. Mongols do worse than other imbeciles in stereognostic recognition tasks and in drawing tests.
5. Mongols and non-mongoloid imbeciles do not seem to differ in their visual perception, nor in the extent and duration with which they are alerted by visual stimuli.
6. The experimental results can be explained in terms of hypotonia and lack of kinesthetic feedback in the mongols.

CHAPTER IX

THEORETICAL AND PRACTICAL
IMPLICATIONS

"THINKING", says Bartlett (1958)' 'is not simply the description either by perception or by recall of something which is there, it is the use of information about something present, to get somewhere else." The sequence of the thought process thus involves intake of relevant information, the filling of gaps either through utilizing cues in the stimulus situation or through some other source, and the directed moving through interconnected steps to a terminus. Though constricted, neither the direction, succession or number of steps taken, nor indeed the terminal point reached need be the same in all cases. What then have the experiments described in previous chapters revealed about deficits and impairments in this sequence? Firstly, the abilities involved in the interpretation of sensory stimuli are certainly inadequate. Impaired discrimination may be due to lack of focusing on the relevant feature of a display. The deficit does not seem to be a perceptual one, but lies in some aspect of discrimination learning which in normals undergoes development during childhood and adolescence. In the severely subnormal the development of the signalling aspect of percepts is deficient.

Hebb thinks that while in adults shape perception and identification may occur at a glance, visual tracing and exploration of outline is necessary for children. Our results about the difference between normal children and normal adults in the ability to discriminate between complex shapes is in accordance with this. The findings that the imbecile has better stereognostic discrimination ability than visual shape recognition, could be explained on similar lines. While we assumed that tracing the outline of the figures occurred in the stereognostic tasks, such detailed exploration may have been absent in the visual conditions. Though the eye movement data showed more movements in subnormals than in normals, these movements were not recorded in conditions where detailed tracing of visual patterns was involved.

On the basis of our experimental results it seems that imbeciles make as many mistakes as children of like mental age when they are asked to discriminate between visual stimuli after only one or two presentations. As far as simple shapes are concerned their speed of visual information intake is not particularly impaired, though Tyson (1961) seems to have found a perceptual speed factor, discriminating between normals and subnormals where complex figures were concerned. However, imbeciles need a longer time and more presentations than normals of like mental age, until they begin to learn to discriminate consistently between stimuli. We have shown that this learning difficulty can at least be partly overcome by the manner in which the task is presented and the response demanded. Increasing dimensions of variability between stimuli as in the word learning experiment, or making verbal coding part of the task, improves discrimination learning, as does simple and continued practice on similar tasks with different constituents.

We don't wish to suggest that lack of verbal facility is solely responsible for impaired discrimination learning. However, it may be said that as the limitation of speech impinges on naming, so perceptual discrimination is also limited. In this way, for example, our design for the touch discrimination experiment permitted us to demonstrate that the absence of appropriate verbal labels attachable to the shapes, prevented cross modality coding of the Greek letters. At present this seems to us to be a likely hypothesis.

The relevance of this process can easily be extended. For example, the reversal of different sized squares presented no difficulty until verbal labels were attached when it needed more trials. The subsequent set of experiments concerning cross modal learning showed how speech coding was of considerable importance in improving scores. Mein and O'Connor (1960) indicated the relatively limited vocabulary of institutionalized imbeciles, and Lyle (1959) reports similar findings.

It must be said that we do not yet know whether the improvement of the extent of imbecile vocabulary would result in improved performance or not. The reason for this is the difficulty which they seem to have in using words even when these are available to them. This absence of the directional function of language so often emphasized by Soviet psychologists, has been confirmed in our experiments. The mechanisms of this are obscure and need further investigation. It seems likely that whatever causes this impediment limits imbecile cognitive development. Obviously environmental and educational attempts should be made to improve speech, and Lyle's data suggest that this could be done. Without some enlargement of verbal conceptualization the imbecile is unlikely to be much assisted in the use of associative capacity. Of course, as we have said before, acquisition of language would not in itself restore complete normality of mental function.

Part of the defective's lack of capacity to handle symbols comes from a reluctance to use them. When forced to do so, as in our inter-modal experiments, imbeciles improved their performance over situations in which they were not obliged to do so. A verbal disinclination as well as a verbal disability seems to be present.

Luria's view about a lack of association between the verbal system and the one governing motor behaviour has been confirmed in many of our experiments. It seems, however, that the prediction that this dissociation can hardly be overcome may be somewhat too pessimistic a view. If coding becomes an unavoidable feature of the task, performance is generally improved. Thus while it is true that fewer words are available to subnormal than to normal children it seems more relevant in our context that they do not tend to use these words spontaneously as mental tools. In our experiments the subnormal children seemed less impaired in tasks concerned with the semantic connection between words, than they were in others in which coding of words into percepts or vice versa occurred. Such coding activity could be imposed if the task was appropriately presented.

Our results seem to be in agreement with Piaget's theories, that logic in linguistic structure does not necessarily imply logic in other operations. The efficiency of a verbal code depends on the connections which relate words and sentences not only to each other but to things and events. Efficient verbal coding depends upon factors other than purely contextual interverbal connections. It depends on the ability to translate events and things readily into images, symbols and signs without changing their meaning.

Subnormal children do not readily use words as a code in this manner even if they do know them. We have tried to demonstrate how stimulus situations can be presented in such a way that they encourage and enforce such coding. It is the determination of the factors which facilitate this process that further experiments must accomplish.

While logic in linguistic structure does not necessarily imply logic in other operations, the converse is also often true. Absence of verbal concepts does not necessarily entail an inability to use such concepts operationally. We have shown that imbeciles do in fact use concepts and categories in sorting tasks. Our results as well as those of Tizard and Loos (1954), Barnett and Cantor (1957) and Clarke and Blakemore (1961) have also shown that principles of classification are readily transferred to similar problems. As in the acquisition of motor skills, it is the initial stages of more complex learning tasks which are most difficult for the imbeciles. A set, or expectancy of what is required by the task, may take a long time to build up, and without such a set many trials may be needed before attention is focused on the relevant aspect of a situation or a display. It is only then that proper learning commences, and subsequent similar tasks are usually learned very much faster. Hebb (1949) expresses this by suggesting that in normals stimuli are organized into phase sequences, which in turn anticipate and influence the intake of further information. Bruner (1957) expresses a similar point of view when he says that in coding information the organism continuously goes beyond the information given. "It is not simply that organisms code the events of their environment, but that they utilize cues for doing so that allow an opportunity for prior adjustment to the event identified."

Thus one positive aspect in cognitive abilities of the severely subnormal seems to be that once the relevant information has been extracted from a display it is available for use in subsequent situations. Furthermore such information, once it has been acquired, is relatively well remembered. The imbecile has at least a limited ability "to go beyond the direct information given" and supply learned and remembered information not given in the immediate stimulus display.

The amount of material which is remembered is not always a

function of the initial number of stimulus presentations. It is the degree of learning or over-learning which determines memory. It will be remembered that in one investigation experimental and control groups differed in the number of trials needed to learn to criterion. Yet the subsequent memory scores between the groups were equal, the subjects who had received more stimulus presentation being no better than those who had had fewer trials. If on the other hand, as in the paired associate learning study, those who had more presentations had actually learned more than those having had fewer trials, then the initial frequency of presentation remains effective in recall.

Vividness of material and the number of alternatives with which a stimulus item was presented were effective for speeding up learning, but not for improving memory. Stimuli which were either more vivid or more intense were sooner identified than the items which were less so. But once these latter had been learned over many trials they were remembered as well as the vivid and intense stimuli.

Thus the evidence points to deficits in acquisition rather than to poor perception, retention or transfer ability. Acquisition seems to be impaired at least partly because of an inability to focus attention on the relevant stimulus features. We are not concerned here with Strauss and Lehtinen's concepts of distractibility and lack of attention in the brain injured child. Rather we want to stress the lack of expectancies and sets appropriate to the task. In other words the imbecile cannot begin to learn until he has found out what precisely it is that he should learn. This latter process may take a long time. The singling out of relevant features of a stimulus display is helped by naming, labelling and the use of verbal coding. We have shown that such verbal coding does not frequently occur spontaneously with imbeciles. Even if they do know the relevant words they tend not to use them as mental tools. We have also shown that this deficit may at least be partly overcome by making coding an intrinsic part of the task.

There is one other point which is relevant to the precise analysis of the learning difficulty. Ellis in an unpublished report suggests that diminished activity in reverberating circuits may represent the neural basis for slow acquisition in mental defectives. Following

Hebb he postulates that such circuits, which are activated by sensory events, may account for immediate memory. The extent or number of these circuits could be reduced by abnormal structure or development of the cortex. Ellis cites our findings on duration of alpha blocking in support of his theory, and suggests that a significant correlation should obtain between alpha blocking duration and behaviour which depends on short term memory rather than learning or long term retention. In fact we have found that the effect of increasing the interval between a warning and a reaction time signal was more marked in some imbeciles, particularly mongols, than in normals (Hermelin and Berkson, unpublished study). Although both groups became slower as time intervals increased, there was relatively more slowing down in the imbeciles. We concluded from this that short duration stimuli activated severely subnormal subjects for a shorter time than normals. This would account for the low level of responsiveness in imbeciles, which is evident in psychological as well as physiological measures. It would point to a need for more and stronger stimulation than is necessary for normal children. When we compared the effects of intensity and frequency of stimulus presentation, those subjects who had failed to learn to criterion after the specified number of trials were not included in subsequent retention tasks. Significantly more subjects from the lower than from the higher intensity conditions had to be excluded.

We have already drawn attention to the nature of the association between a low state of arousal, hypotonia and lack of responsiveness. Differences between mongol and non-mongol imbeciles have been attributed to these mechanisms. Similar processes may be responsible for the slow utilization of stimuli, and impairment in acquisition in imbeciles when compared with normals.

The low level of responsiveness may account for general inhibition and lack of "output" rather than impairment in "input" mechanisms. The effects of this would be evident in many activities, including speech behaviour, and such a view is supported by Lyle's (1959) findings about lower verbal ability scores of mongols than of non-mongol imbeciles. It is also supported within broad limits by the results of Berkson's reaction time experiments, as well as by the difference which we find between normals and defectives in the level of psychological arousal measure in response to simple stimuli. It will be remembered that the change in skin potential and the duration of alpha blocking after a light flash was significantly greater in the normals. Difficulties in response output seem particularly indicated in the mongol. Because of general hypotonia there is less psycho-physiological responsiveness to simple stimuli, slower motor reactions and less kinesthetic feedback as shown in their stereognostic and drawing disabilities.

It seems to us that these findings have some practical implications for the treatment of cognitive defects in severely subnormal children. The diminished responsiveness to stimuli as well as the lack of perception of signal quality in percepts would indicate the need for presentation of educational aids and displays which are quantitatively as well as qualitatively distinct from those used for normals. Presentation of material at relatively high intensity levels, stressing of relevant aspects of stimuli and sufficient frequency of presentation are all necessary for the severely subnormal child if he is to begin to learn. Imbeciles should also be taught to verbalize while carrying out motor tasks as in our reversal experiment.

Though most of the findings would be in accord with the views of Luria or House and Zeaman we have refrained from interpreting them in the light of any one single theory. The main reason for this is that low grade deficiency is not unitary in its pattern of functional deficits and both the aetiology as well as the nature and degree of central nervous impairment are extremely diverse. Therefore attempts at general theorizing against a background of a multitude of ill-understood conditions would seem to us premature. Our own contribution consists in emphasizing deficits in acquisition and coding which we consider more important and marked than those in retention and transfer. The deficiency in coding consists in an inability to associate words and signs or words and percepts. We have also shown how some situations facilitate coding and in addition have indicated the possibility of differential deficit in diagnostic subgroups. We would stress finally the tentative rather than conclusive character of the studies reported and point out the need for many more investigations before even the limited conclusions presented above would seem to be well established. In studying mental function in the severely

I

subnormal, we have used throughout the techniques and methods developed in experimental psychology with normal subjects. The inferences which can be made from our studies may in turn be applicable to the appropriate areas of normal cognitive processes.

REFERENCES

ALEXANDER, W. P. (1935) Intelligence, concrete and abstract. *Brit. J. Psychol. Monogr. Suppl.*, No. 19.

ANANIEV, B. G. (1961) The theory of the sense of touch. In *Recent Soviet Psychology*. N. O'Connor (Ed.), London: Pergamon Press.

ANNETT, J. (1957) The information capacity of young mental defectives in an assembly task. *J. ment. Sci.*, **103**, 621–631.

ATTNEAVE, F. (1954) Some informational aspects of visual perception. *Psychol. Rev.*, **61**, 183–193.

BALLARD, P. B. (1913) Oblivescence and reminiscence. *Brit. J. Psychol. Monogr. Suppl.*, **1**, No. 2, 564–566.

BARNETT, C. D. and CANTOR, G. N. (1957) Discrimination set in defectives. *Amer. J. ment. Def.*, **62**, 334–337.

BARNETT, C. D., ELLIS, N. R. and PRYER, MARGARET W. (1960,a) Learning in familial and brain-injured defectives. *Amer. J. ment. Def.*, **65**, 51–58.

BARNETT, C. D., ELLIS, N. R. and PRYER, MARGARET W. (1960,b) Serial positions effects in superior and retarded subjects. *Psychol. Rep.*, **7**, 111113 .

BARTLETT, F. (1958) *Thinking: An Experimental and Social Study*. London: Allen & Unwin.

BERKSON, G. (1960,a) An analysis of reaction time in normal and mentally deficient young men. I. Duration threshold experiment. *J. ment. Def. Res.*, **4**, 51–58.

BERKSON, G. (1960,b) An analysis of reaction time in normal and mentally deficient young men. II. Variation of complexity in reaction time tasks. *J. ment. Def. Res.*, **4**, 59–67.

BERKSON, G. (1960,c) An analysis of reaction time in normal and mentally deficient young men. III. Variation of stimulus and of response complexity. *J. ment. Def. Res.*, **4**, 69–77.

BERKSON, G. (1961) Responsiveness of the mentally deficient. *Amer. J. ment. Def.*, **66**, 277–286.

BERKSON, G. and CANTOR, G. N. (1960) A study of mediation in mentally retarded and normal school children. *J. Educ. Psychol.*, **51**, 82–86.

BERKSON, G., HERMELIN, BEATE and O'CONNOR, N. (1961) Physiological responses of normals and institutionalized mental defectives to repeated stimuli. *J. ment. def. Res.*, **5**, 30–39.

BERNHAUT, M., GELLHORN, E. and RASMUSSEN, A. T. (1953) Experimental contributions to problems of consciousness. *J. Neurophysiol.*, **16**, 21–35.

111

BEXTON, W. H., HERON, W. and SCOTT, T. H. (1954) Effects of decreased variation in the sensory environment. *Canad. J. Psychol.*, **8**, 70–76.

BINET, A. and SIMON, T. (1914) *The Mentally Defective Child.* (Trans. W. B. Drummond.) New York: Longmans Green.

BINET, A., SIMON, T. and VANEY, F. A. (1907) Pedagogie scientifique, *L'Annee Psychologique*, **12**, 233–274.

BIRCH, J. W. and MATHEWS, J. (1951) The hearing of mental defectives: its measurement and characteristics. *Amer. J. ment. def.*, **55**, 384–393.

BLACKETER-SIMMONDS, L. D. A. (1953) An investigation into the supposed differences existing between mongols and other mentally defective subjects with regard to certain psychological traits. *J. ment. Sci.*, **99**, 702–719.

BROGDEN, W. J. and SMITH, R. E. (1954) The effect of number of choices per unit of a verbal maze on learning and serial position order. *J. exp. Psychol.*, **47**, 235-240.

BRUNER, J. S. (1957) *Contemporary Approaches to Cognition.* Cambridge: Harvard Univ. Press.

BRUNER, J. S., GOODNOW, J. J. and AUSTEN, G. A. (1956) *A Study of Thinking.* New York: Wiley.

BURROUGHS, G. E. R. (1957) *A Study of the Vocabulary of Young Children.* Birmingham Univ. Inst. Educ. Monogrs. 1. Edinburgh: Oliver & Boyd.

BURT, C. (1926) in *The Education of the Adolescent.* (Hadow Report.) Board of Education Reports, London, H.M.S.O., Appendix.

BURT, C. (1937) *The Backward Child.* (4th Ed.), London: Univ. London Press. Rev. Ed. 1946.

CANTOR, G. N. and HOTTEL, J. V. (1955) Discrimination learning in mental defectives as a function of magnitude of food reward and intelligence level. *Amer. J. ment. Def.*, **60**, 380–384.

CARTER, C. O. (1958) A life-table for mongols with the causes of death. *J. ment. def. Res.*, **2**, 64–74.

CASSEL, R. H. (1949) Design reproduction in mental deficiency. *J. consult. Psychol.*, **13**, 425-428.

CLARIDGE, G. S. and O'CONNOR, N. (1957) The relationship between incentive personality type and improvement in performance of imbeciles. *J. ment. def. Res.*, **1**, 16–25.

CLARKE, A. D. B. (1958) The abilities and trainability of imbeciles, in *Mental Deficiency: the Changing Outlook.* Clarke, A. D. B. & Clarke, Ann (Eds.), London: Methuen.

CLARKE, A. D. B. and BLAKEMORE, C. B. (1961) Age and perceptual motor transfer in imbeciles. *Brit. J. Psychol.*, **52**, 125–132.

CLARKE, A. D. B. and COOKSON, MARGARET (1962) Perceptual motor transfer in imbeciles: A second series of experiments. *Brit. J. Psychol.*, **53**, 321–330.

COFER, C. N. and FOLEY, J. P. (1942) Mediated generalization and the interpretation of verbal behaviour. *Psychol. Rev.*, **49**, 6, 513–540.

COLLMAN, R. D. (1931) *The Psychogalvanic Reactions of Exceptional and*

Normal School Children. Contributions to Educ. No. 469. New York: Teachers College.

COLLMAN, R. D. (1959) The galvanic skin responses of mentally retarded and other children in England. *Amer. J. ment. Def.,* **63,** 626–632.

COX, D. R. (1958) Regression analysis of binary sequences. *J. Roy. Stat. Soc. (B),* **20,** 216–242, Example 3, p. 225.

CROSSMAN, E. R. F. W. (1955) The measurement of discriminability. *Quart. J. exp. Psychol.,* **7,** 176–195.

DAVIS, R. A. and MOORE, C. C. (1935) Methods of measuring retention. *J. gen. Psychol.* **12,** 144–155.

DAVIS, R. C. (1940) *Set and Muscular Tension.* Indiana: Indiana Univ. Public. Scientific Services. **10.**

DEINNINGER, R. L. and FITTS, P. M. (1955) Stimulus-response Compatibility information theory and perceptual motor performance, in Quastler, H. (Ed.) *Information Theory in Psychology.* Glencoe, Illinois: Free Press Publishers.

DESCOEUDRES, A. (1928) *The Education of Mentally Defective Children.* London: Harrap.

DISTIFANO, M. K. and SLOAN, W. (1958) Motor proficiency in mental defectives. *Percept. and Motor Skills,* **8,** 231–234.

DUNCAN, J. (1942) *The Education of the Ordinary Child.* London: Nelson.

ELLIS, N. R., BARNETT, C. D. and PRYER, MARGARET W. (1959). Operant Behaviour in Mental Defectives: Exploratory Studies. Pineville State Colony Annual *Report* 1. *Behavioural Studies in Mental Deficiency,* 72–77.

ELLIS, N. R., PRYER, MARGARET W. and BARNETT, C. D. (1959) Motor Learning and Retention in Normals and Defectives. Pineville State Colony Annual *Report* 1. *Behavioural Studies in Mental Deficiency,* 58–71.

ELLIS, N. R. and SLOAN, W. (1957) The relationship between intelligence and simple reaction time in mental defectives. *Percept. and Motor Skills,* **7,** 65–67.

ELLIS, N. R. and SLOAN, W. (1957) The relationship between intelligence and skin conductance. *Amer. J. ment. Def.,* **63,** 304–306.

FITTS, P. M. and DEINNINGER, R. L. (1954) S-R compatibility: Correspondence among paired elements within stimulus and response codes. *J. exp. Psychol.,* **48,** 483–492.

FITTS, P. M. and SEEGER, C. M. (1953) S-R compatibility: spacial characteristics of stimulus and response codes. *J. exp. Psychol.,* **46,** 199–210.

FREEMAN, J. L. and SIMPSON, R. M. (1938) Skin esistancer and muscular tension. *J. gen. Psychol.,* **19,** 319–325.

GARDNER, L. P. (1945) The learning of low-grade aments. *Amer. J. ment. Def.,* **50,** 59–80.

GENTRY, J., KAPLAN, S. T. and ISCOE, TRA (1956) Studies in abstractive generalization: comparisons between various human age groups and monkeys on similar learning tasks. School Avn. Med., U.S.A.F., Randolph A.F.B., Texas, 55–83.

GOLDSTEIN, K. and SCHEERER, M. (1941) Abstract and concrete behaviour: An experimental study with special tests. *Psychol. Monogr.* 53, No. 2.

GORDON, H. M. (1944) Some aspects of sensory discrimination in mongolism. *Amer. J. ment. Def.*, **49**, 55–63.

GORDON, S., O'CONNOR, N. and TIZARD, J. (1954) Some effects of incentives on the performance of imbeciles. *Brit. J. Psychol.*, **45**, 277–287.

GRIFFITHS, B. C., SPITZ, H. H. and LIPMAN, R. S. (1959) Verbal mediation and concept formation in retarded and normal subjects. *J. exp. Psychol.*, **58**, 247–251.

HALPIN, V. G. (1955) Rotation errors made by brain injured and familial children in two motor tests. *Amer. J. ment. Def.*, **59**, 485–489.

HAUN, K. W. (1960) Measures of association and verbal learning. *Psychol. Reports*, **7**, 451–460.

HARLOW, H. F. (1949) The formation of learning sets. *Psychol. Rev.*, **56**, 51–65.

HEBB, D. O. (1949) *The Organization of Behaviour.* New York: Wiley.

HEBB, D. O. (1958) *A Textbook of Psychology*, London: Saunders.

HEIDBREDER, E. F. (1928) Problem solving in children and adults. *J. genet. Psychol.*, **35**, 522–545.

HERMELIN, BEATE (1958) *Concept Learning and Verbalization in Imbeciles.* Ph.D. Thesis, University of London.

HERMELIN, BEATE and O'CONNOR, N. (1958) The rote and concept learning of imbeciles. *J. ment. def. Res.*, **2**, 21–27.

HERMELIN, BEATE and O'CONNOR, N. (1960,a) Reading ability of severely subnormal children. *J. ment. def. Res.*, **4**, 144–147.

HERMELIN, BEATE and O'CONNOR, N. (1960,b) Like and cross modality responses in normal and subnormal children. *Quart. J. exp. Psychol.*, **12**, 48–53.

HERMELIN, BEATE and O'CONNOR, N. (1961,a) Recognition of shapes by normal and subnormal children. *Brit. J. Psychol.*, **52**, 281–284.

HERMELIN, BEATE and O'CONNOR, N. (1961,b) Shape perception and reproduction in normal children and mongol and non-mongol imbeciles. *J. ment. def. Res.*, **5**, 67–71.

HOUSE, BETTY J. and ZEAMAN, D. (1958) Visual discrimination learning in imbeciles. *Amer. J. ment. Def.*, **63**, 447–452.

HOUSE, BETTY J. and ZEAMAN, D. (1959,a) Position discrimination and reversal in low-grade retardates. *J. Comp. & Physiol. Psychol.*, **52**, 564–565.

HOUSE, BETTY J. and ZEAMAN, D. (1959,b) Discrimination learning in retardates. *Traing. School Bull.*, **56**, 62–67.

HOUSE, BETTY J. and ZEAMAN, D. (1960,a) Transfer of a discrimination from objects to patterns. *J. exp. Psychol.*, **59**, 298–302.

HOUSE, BETTY J. and ZEAMAN, D. (1960,b) Visual discrimination learning and intelligence in defectives of low mental age. *Amer. J. ment. Def.*, **65**, 51–58.

References 115

House, Betty J., Zeaman, D., Orlando, R. and W. Fischer, (1957) Learning and transfer in mental defectives. Progress Rep. No. 1, NIMH, USPHS, Res. Grant 1099 to Univ. Connecticut, 58–63.

Hovland, C. I. (1938) Experimental studies in rote-learning theory: 1. Reminiscence following learning by massed and by distributed practice. *J. exp. Psychol.*, **22**, 201–224.

Hull, C. L. (1920) Quantitative aspects of the evolution of concepts. *Psychol. Monogr.*, **28**.

Humphrey, G. (1948) *Directed Thinking*. New York: Dodd, Mead.

Ingham, J. (1952) Memory and intelligence. *Brit. J. Psychol.*, **43**, 20–31.

Inhelder, Bärbel (1955) De la configuration perceptive à la structure operatoire. *Bull. de Psychologie*, **i**, 6–20.

Inhelder, Bärbel and Piaget, J. (1958) *The Growth of Logical Thinking from Childhood to Adolescence*. London: Routledge and Kegan Paul.

Iscoe, Ira and Giller, D. (1959) Areas of concept formation in the mentally retarded. *Amer. J. ment. Def.*, **63**, 112–115.

Itard, J. M. G. (1801) *The Wild Boy of Aveyron*. Trans. G. & M. Humphrey (1932). New York: Appleton Century.

Johnson, D. M. (1955) *The Psychology of Thought and Judgment*. Gardner Murphy (Ed.). New York: Harper & Bros.

Kennedy, J. L. and Travis, R. C. (1947) Prediction of speed of performance by muscle action potentials. *Science*, **105**, 410–411.

Kirk, S. A. (1960) The effects of educational procedures on the development of retarded children. *Proceedings of the London Conference on the Scientific Aspects of Mental Deficiency*. London: May & Baker.

Kirk, S. A. and McCarthy, J. J. (1961) The Illinois test of psycholinguistic abilities—an approach to differential diagnosis. *Amer. J. ment. Def.*, **66**, 399–412.

Kounin, J. S. (1948) Experimental studies of rigidity. I. The measurement of rigidity in normal and feebleminded persons. II. The explanatory power of the concept of rigidity as applied to feeblemindedness. *Character & Pers.*, **9**, 273–282.

Krueger, W. C. F. (1929) J. exp. Psychol., 12, 71–78, quoted in Woodworth R. S. *Experimental Psychology*, 1946, New York: Henry Holt (p. 58).

Kuhlmann, F. (1904) Experimental studies in mental deficiency. *Amer. J. Psychol.*, **15**, 391–446.

Lacey, J. I. and Smith, R. L. (1954) Conditioning and generalization of unconscious anxiety. *Science*, **120**, No. 3130, 1045–1052.

Leonard, A. (1955) Factors which influence channel capacity, in Quastler, H. (Ed.). *Information Theory in Psychology*. Glencoe, Illinois: Free Press Publishers.

Liublinskaya, A. A. (1957) The role of language in the development of a child's perceptual activity, in Simon, B. (Ed.) *Psychology in the Soviet Union*, London: Routledge & Kegan Paul.

Luria, A. R. (1958) Dynamic approach to the mental development of the abnormal child. *J. ment. def. Res.*, **2**, 37–52.

LURIA, A. R. (1959,a) Experimental study of the higher nervous activity of the abnormal child. *J. ment. def. Res.*, **3**, 1–22.

LURIA, A. R. (1959,b) The directing function of speech in development and dissolution, I. *Word*, **15**, 341–352.

LURIA, A. R. (1959,c) The directive function of speech in development and dissolution, II. *Word*, **15**, 453–464.

LURIA, A. R. (1961) *The Role of Speech in the Regulation of Normal and Abnormal Behaviour.* London: Pergamon Press.

LURIA, A. R. and VINOGRADOVA, OLGA S. (1959) An objective investigation of the dynamics of semantic systems. *Brit. J. Psychol.*, **50**, 89–105.

LYLE, J. G. (1959) The effect of an institution environment upon verbal development of imbecile children. I. Verbal intelligence. *J. ment. def. Res.*, **3**, 122–128.

LYLE, J. G. (1960) The effect of an institution environment upon the verbal development of imbecile children. III. The Brooklands residential family unit. *J. ment. def. Res.*, **4**, 14–22.

MARG, E. (1951) Development of electro-oculography. *Arch. Ophthalm.*, **45**, 169–185.

McCULLOCH, T. L., RESWICK, J. and ROY, I. (1955) Studies of word learning in mental defectives. I. Effects of mental level and age. *Amer. J. ment. Def.*, **60**, 133–139.

McFIE, J. (1961) Recent advances in phrenology. *Lancet*, **ii**, 360–363.

McPHERSON, MARION W. (1947) A summary of experimental studies of learning in individuals who achieve subnormal ratings on standardized psychometric measures. *Amer. J. ment. Def.*, **52**, 232–254.

McPHERSON, MARION W. (1958) Learning and mental deficiency. *Amer. J. ment. Def.*, **62**, 870–877.

MEIN, R. (1961) A study of the oral vocabularies of severely subnormal patients. *J. ment. def. Res.*, **5**, 52–59.

MEIN, R. and O'CONNOR, N. (1960) A study of the oral vocabularies of severely subnormal patients. *J. ment. def. Res.*, **4**, 130–143.

MESCHERIAKOV, A. I. (1953) *Breakdown in the Interaction of the Two Signal Systems in the Formation of Simple Motor Reactions in Cases of Local Injury to the Brain.* Thesis: Moscow University.

MILLER, G. A. (1951) *Language and Communication.* New York: McGraw-Hill.

MILLER, G. A. (1956) The magical number seven, plus or minus two: some limits on our capacity for processing information. *Psychol. Rev.*, **63**, 81–97.

MONTESSORI, M. (1912) *Montessori Method.* Trans. A. F. George. New York: F. A. Stokes.

MOWRER, O. H. (1950) *Learning Theory and Personality Dynamics.* New York: The Ronald Press.

NEPOMNYASHCHAYA, N. I. (1956) Some conditions of the derangement of the regulating role of speech in oligophrenic children. In *Problems of Higher Nervous Activity of Normal and Abnormal Children.* A. R. Luria (Ed.) Moscow: Academy of Pedagogical Sciences.

O'CONNOR, N. (1957) Imbecility and colour blindness. *Amer. J. ment. Def.*, **62**, 83–87.

O'CONNOR, N. (1958,a) Learning and mental defect. In *Mental Deficiency: The Changing Outlook.* Clarke, A. D. B. and Clarke, Ann. (Eds.). London: Methuen.

O'CONNOR, N. (1958,b) Brain damage and mental defect. In *Mental Deficiency: The Changing Outlook.* Clarke, A. D. B. and Clarke, Ann (Eds.). London: Methuen.

O'CONNOR, N. and CLARIDGE, G. (1958) A "Crespi Effect" in male imbeciles. *Brit. J. Psychol.*, **49**, 42–48.

O'CONNOR, N. and HERMELIN, BEATE (1959,a) Some effects of word learning in imbeciles. *Language and Speech*, **2**, 63–71.

O'CONNOR, N. and HERMELIN, BEATE (1959,b) Discrimination and reversal learning in imbeciles. *J. ab. soc. Psychol.*, **59**, 409–413.

O'CONNOR, N. and HERMELIN, BEATE (1961,a) Like and cross modality recognition in subnormal children. *Quart. J. exp. Psychol.*, **13**, 48–52.

O'CONNOR, N. and HERMELIN, BEATE (1961,b) Visual and stereognostic shape recognition in normal children and mongol and non-mongol imbeciles. *J. ment. def. Res.*, **5**, 63–66.

O'CONNOR, N. and HERMELIN, BEATE (1962) Recall in normals and subnormals of like mental age. *J. abn. soc. Psychol.* (In press.)

O'CONNOR, N. and VENABLES, P. H. (1956) A note on the basal level of skin conductance and Binet I.Q. *Brit. J. Psychol.*, **47**, 148–149.

ORDAHL, L. F. and ORDAHL, G. (1915) Qualitative differences between level of intelligence in feebleminded children. *J. Psycho-Asthenics, Monogr. Sup.*, **1**, 3–50.

OSGOOD, C. E. (1953) *Method and Theory in Experimental Psychology.* New York: Oxford University Press.

OSGOOD, C. E., SUCI, G. J. and TANNENBAUM, P. H. (1957) *The Measurement of Meaning.* Urbana: Illinois Univ. Press.

PASCAL, G. R., STOLUROW, L. M., ZABARENKO, R. N. and CHAMBERS, C. S. (1951) The delayed reaction in mental defectives. *Amer. J. ment. Def.*, **56**, 152–160.

PENROSE, L. S. (1949) *The Biology of Mental Defect.* London: Sidgwick & Jackson. (Revised Edition, 1954).

PIAGET, J. (1930) *The Child's Conception of Physical Causality.* New York: Harcourt Brace.

PIAGET, J. (1955) *The Child's Construction of Reality.* London: Routledge.

PIAGET, J. (1961) *Les Mecanismes Perceptifs.* Paris: Presse Universitaire de France.

PICKFORD, R. W. (1951) *Individual Differences in Colour Vision.* London: Routledge & Kegan Paul.

PILLSBURY, W. B. and RAUSH, H. L. (1943) An extension of the Köhler-Restorff inhibition phenomenon. *Amer. J. Psychol.*, **56**, 293–298.

PLENDERLEITH, M. (1956) Discrimination learning and discrimination reversal learning in normal and feebleminded children. *J. genet. Psychol.*, **88**, 107–112.

RAZRAN, G. H. S. (1939) A quantitative study of meaning by a conditioned salivary technique (semantic conditioning). *Science*, **90**, 89–90.

RIESS, B. F. (1946) Genetic changes in semantic conditioning. *J. exp. Psychol.*, **36**, 143–152.

RUCH, T. C., FULTON, J. F. and GERMAN, W. J. (1938) Sensory discrimination in monkey, chimpanzee and man, after lesions of the parietal lobe. *Arch. Neurol. Psychiat. Chicago*, **39**, 919–937.

ROLLIN, H. R. (1946) Personality in mongolism with special reference to the incidence of catatonic psychosis. *Amer. J. ment. Def.*, **51**, 219–237.

SAMUELS, INA (1959) Reticular mechanisms and behaviour. *Psychol. Bull.*, **56**, 1–25.

SARASON, S. B. (1953) *Psychological Problems in Mental Deficiency*. New York: Harper.

SCHWARZ, L. A. (1948) Knowledge of the word and its sound form as a conditioned stimulus. *Bull. exp. Biol. Med.*, **25**, 292–4: **27**, 412–15.

SEGUIN, E. (1846) *Traitement Moral, Hygiene et Education des Idiots et des Autres Enfants Arriérés*. Paris: J. B. Ballière.

SEGUIN, E. (1866) *Idiocy and its Treatment by the Physiological Method.* Reprinted. Tchrs. College, Columbia, 1907.

SHACKEL, B. (1960) A pilot study in electro-oculography. *Brit. J. Ophthalm.*, **44**, 89–113.

SKEELS, H. M. (1938) Mental development of children in foster homes. *J. consult. Psychol.*, **2**, 33–43.

SKINNER, B. F. (1938) *The Behavior of Organisms. An Experimental Analysis*. New York: Appleton Century Crofts.

SLOAN, W. and BERG, J. (1957) A comparison of two types of learning in mental defectives. *Amer. J. ment. Def.*, **61**, 556–566.

SPEARMAN, C. (1927) *The Nature of Intelligence and the Principles of Cognition*. London: Macmillan.

SPIKER, C., GERYNOY, J. R. and SHEPARD, W. O. (1956) Children's concepts of middle-sizedness and performance of the intermediate size problem. *J. Occ. Psychol.*, **79**, 416–419.

STAATS, A. W. and STAATS, CAROLYN K. (1958) Meaning and (M) correlated but separate. *Tech. Rep. No. 7*: Contract No. 2305 (00).

STAATS, CAROLYN K. and STAATS, A. W. (1957) Meaning established by classical conditioning. *J. exp. Psychol.*, **54**, 74–80.

STEBBING, L. SUSAN (1948) *Thinking to Some Purpose*. London: Penguin Books.

STEVENSON, H. W. and ISCOE, I. (1955) Transposition in the feebleminded. *J. exp. Psychol.*, **49**, 11–15.

STEVENSON, H. W. and ZIEGLER, E. F. (1957) Discrimination learning and rigidity in normal and feebleminded individuals. The Univ. of Texas, Unpublished report.

STRAUSS, A. A. and KEPHART, N. C. (1955) *Psychopathology and Education of the Brain Injured Child.* Vol. II, *Progress in Theory and Clinic.* New York: Grune & Stratton.

STRAUSS, A. A. and LEHTINEN, L. E. (1947) *Psychopathology and Education of the Brain Injured Child.* New York: Grune & Stratton.

THOMPSON, C. W. and MAGARET, A. (1947) Differential test responses of normals and mental defectives. *J. ab. soc. Psychol.,* **42,** 285–293.

THOMSON, G. H. (1939) *The Factorial Analysis of Human Ability.* London: Univ. London Press.

THORNDIKE, E. L. (1911) *Animal Intelligence.* New York: Macmillan.

THOULESS, R. H. (1953) *Straight and Crooked Thinking.* London: Pan Books.

THURSTONE, L. L. (1943) *Primary Mental Abilities.* Psychometric Monographs 1.

TIKHOMIROVA, O. K. (1956) Verbal regulation of movements in oligophrenic children under a conflict between verbal and direct signals. In *Problems of Higher Nervous Activity in Normal and Abnormal Children.* A. R. Luria (Ed.). Moscow: Academy of Pedagogical Sciences.

TIZARD, J. (1960) *The Residential Care of Mentally Handicapped Children.* Proceedings of London Conference on the Scientific Aspects of Mental Deficiency. London: May & Baker.

TIZARD, J. and LOOS, F. M. (1954) The learning of a spatial relations test by adult imbeciles. *Amer. J. ment. Def.,* **59,** 1, 85–90.

TREDGOLD, A. F. (1952) *A Text Book of Mental Deficiency.* London: Ballière Tindall & Cox.

TYSON, MOYA C. (1961) *A Comparison of the Abilities of Normal and Subnormal Children to Match and Discriminate Figures.* Ph.D. Thesis, Univ. London.

UNDERWOOD, B. J. and RICHARDSON, J. (1956) Some verbal materials for the study of concept formation. *Psychol. Bull.,* **53,** 84–95.

VERNON, P. E. (1950) *The Structure of Human Abilities.* London: Methuen.

VIGOTSKY, L. S. (1939) Thought and speech. *Psychiatry,* **2,** 29–54.

VINACKE, W. (1952) *The Psychology of Thinking.* New York: McGraw-Hill.

VON RESTORFF, H. (1933) Über die Wirkung von Bereichsbildungen im Spurenfeld (In W. Köhler and H. von Restorff, Analyse von Vorgängen im Spurenfeld). *Psychol. Forsch.,* **18,** 299–342.

WEINSTEIN, B. (1945) The evolution of intelligent behaviour in Rhesus monkeys. *Genet. Psychol. Monog.,* **31.**

WHITESIDE, S. (1934) Spontaneity of normal and mentally defective subjects in selective learning. *Proceedings of the Amer. Ass. for ment. Def.,* **39,** 344–383.

WILLIAMS, O. (1926) A study of the phenomenon of reminiscence. *J. exp. Psychol.,* **9,** 368–387.

WOODROW, H. (1946) The ability to learn. *Psychol. Rev.,* **53,** 147–158.

WOODWARD, MARY (1959) The behaviour of idiots interpreted by Piaget's

120   *Speech and Thought in Severe Subnormality*

theory of sensory-motor development. *Brit. J. Educ. Psychol.*, **29,** 60–71.

WOODWORTH, R. S. (1946) *Experimental Psychology.* New York: Henry Holt.

ZANGWILL, O. L. (1960) *Cerebral Dominance and its Relation to Psychological Function.* London: Oliver & Boyd.

ZAPOROZHETS, A. V. (1955) The development of voluntary movements. *Vopros. Psikh.*, No. 1.

ZINCHENKO, V. P. and LOMOV, B. F. (1960) The functions of hand and eye movements in the process of perception. *Problems of Psychology,* **1, 2,** 12–25. London: Pergamon Press.

ZIPF, G. K. (1935) *The Psycho-biology of Language.* Boston: Houghton Mifflin.

INDEX